LOGOS AND
NO GOS

LOGOS AND NO GOS

How to understand and get the most from your brand IP

Geoff Steward

The Chartered
Institute of Marketing

John Wiley & Sons, Ltd

Other Wiley Editorial Offices

Wiley have other editorial offices in the USA, Germany, Australia,
Singapore and Canada.

Wiley also publishes its books in a variety of electronic formats. Some
content that appears in print may not be available in electronic books.

British Library Cataloguing in Publication Data

Steward, Geoff, Solicitor.
   Logos and no gos : how to understand and get the most from your brand
IP / Geoff Steward.
     p. cm.
   Includes bibliographical references and index.
   ISBN-13: 978-0-470-06037-7 (cloth : alk. paper)
   ISBN-10: 0-470-06037-7 (cloth : alk. paper)
   1. Intellectual property–England. I. Title.
   KD1264.S74 2007
   346.4204'88–dc22   2006033497

A catalogue record for this book is available from the British Library

ISBN-13 978-0-470-06037-7 (HB)
ISBN-10 0-470-06037-9 (HB)

Typeset in 11/15pt Trump Mediaeval by SNP Best-set Typesetter Ltd.,
   Hong Kong
Printed and bound in Great Britain by TJ International Ltd, Padstow,
   Cornwall, UK
This book is printed on acid-free paper responsibly manufactured from
   sustainable forestry
in which at least two trees are planted for each one used for paper
   production.

CONTENTS

Preface   xv

About the author   xvii

1   **CREATING AND IDENTIFYING
    YOUR IP**   1

Trade marks   2

*What can you register as a trade
mark?*   2

*What can't you register as a trade
mark?*   4

Always conduct pre-emptive searches   6

Unregistered trade marks   9

Use of the ® and ™ symbols   10

Copyright   12

What is copyright all about?   12

What attracts copyright protection?   13

*What does not attract copyright
protection?*   14

Protecting your ideas   15

*Make sure that you own the
copyright*   15

Period of copyright protection   18

Moral rights   19

Database right   20

What is database right?   20

*What protection does database right
give you?*   21

*In what respect do you need to bother
with database right for the purposes
of your brand strategy?*   22

Designs   23

UK registered designs   24

UK unregistered designs   27

*European Community designs
(registered and unregistered)*   28

*Overlap between trade marks and
designs*   31

*Benefits of registering device marks/
logos as designs*   32

....

2 **REGISTERING YOUR IP** 35

Trade marks 36

The Nice classification system 36

UK registrations 37

Community registrations 44

International registrations 49

The standard Nice classification of goods and services for trade mark registrations (from January 2007) 52

Copyright 71

No UK registration system 71

The international protection available for copyright works 71

Use the © symbol 73

Designs 74

UK registration procedure 74

Community registration procedure 77

3 **HOUSEKEEPING YOUR TRADE MARK PORTFOLIO** 81

Housekeeping tips for preserving and protecting your trade mark portfolio 82

Register your trade marks in the name of the same proprietor 82

Be consistent when using your trade marks   83

Do not allow your trade marks to become generic   86

Conduct regular trade mark audits   87

Certificates   89

Keep accurate and accessible records   89

Renewal dates   91

4 IP AND YOUR EMPLOYEES   93

IP and employees   94

What to include in your employment contracts and why   94

Confidentiality clauses   95

Moral rights and waiver   96

Commissioned works/Contractors   97

Communicating to all employees the importance of IP   98

Chain of command   99

5 EXPLOITATION OF YOUR IP   101

Exploitation of your IP   102

*What is the difference between a
licence and an assignment?* 102

Exclusive/Non-exclusive 104

Registration implications 105

Registrations by rogue licensees 106

*Standard protective licensing
provisions* 107

Franchising 110

Mortgaging/Selling off unused IP 111

6 **POLICING YOUR IP** 113

Policing your IP 114

*Why is it important to monitor your
IP for potential third party
infringements?* 114

*How can you find out if somebody is
infringing your intellectual property
rights?* 114

*Which governmental or public
agencies can help you?* 115

*How can private service providers
help you monitor your intellectual
property for infringements?* 119

7 HOW ARE YOUR IP RIGHTS INFRINGED? 127

Registered trade marks 128

Advantages of registering 128

Acts of civil infringement 128

Criminal trade mark offences 131

The grey market goods problem 132

Copyright 136

Acts of civil infringement 136

Defences to civil copyright infringement 139

Criminal copyright offences 140

Designs 142

UK registered designs 142

UK unregistered designs 144

Compulsory licensing of your unregistered design 147

Community designs (registered and unregistered) 147

Criminal offences 148

8 ENFORCING YOUR IP AND THE REMEDIES AVAILABLE TO YOU   149

How to react to an infringement of your rights   150

Do you have a clear reporting procedure and chain of command?   150

The need for speed   151

The importance of a confusion log   151

Cease and desist letters   153

A word of warning about making unjustified threats   154

Website infringements and service providers   155

What next?   157

Remedies   161

Injunctions   162

Delivery up, recall, seizure and destruction   169

Damages/Account of profits   171

Disclosure of the identity and whereabouts of other wrongdoers and information on infringing products   174

Publication of judicial decisions   175

9   HOW TO AVOID INFRINGING
    OTHER PEOPLE'S IP   177

    How to avoid infringing other
    people's IP   178

10 REGISTERING AND PROTECTING
    YOUR DOMAIN NAMES   183

    Domain names   184

    What is a domain name?   184

    What is the value of a domain name? 184

    Registering a domain name?   184

    *Problems with the registration
    system*   185

    Disputes   187

    Trade mark infringement/passing off 188

    Alternative dispute resolution   189

11 THE TAKE-HOME MESSAGE   195

    The dos and don'ts of brand strategy 196

    Trade mark registrations   196

    Trade mark portfolios   198

    Trade mark infringements   202

    Design registrations   205

CONTENTS

Copyright   207

Database right   210

Domain names   211

Index   213

PREFACE

·····································

Logos and No Gos has been written to help brand
owners design and implement the most effective
strategy to protect their intellectual property
rights and to ensure that they do not inadvertently infringe anyone else's.

Intellectual property is one of the most valuable
assets of all brand owners and is what distin-
guishes them from their competitors in local,
national and global markets. Brand protection
should therefore be a primary concern as it represents a significant proportion of a brand owner's
marketing (and, if things go wrong, legal) budget.
Damage to a brand image can have a direct impact
on a company's bottom line. It is therefore crucial
that brand owners understand how to get
maximum value from and how best to protect
their intellectual property rights.

All brand owners should have a written IP policy
dealing with issues such as what rights the

company owns, who is responsible for looking after them, what the company's licensing policy is and how the company deals with infringers. *Logos and No Gos* is a user-friendly, easy-reference guide, which covers the main areas which brand owning companies need to consider when devising or improving their IP strategy. Each chapter deals with a particular topic from the identification and creation of IP rights to the ultimate enforcement of those rights. As the focus is upon brands, I have not dealt with the complex subject of patents which could form a further guidebook in itself.

I am grateful to all members of the IP Group at Macfarlanes and to Catherine Wolfe and Nicola Shackleton for their invaluable input into this book which I hope you will find useful as a reference tool.

Geoff Steward
Head of Contentious IP
Macfarlanes

ABOUT THE AUTHOR

....

Geoff Steward qualified as a solicitor at Macfarlanes in 1995. In 2002 he became a partner in the Litigation Department and now heads the firm's contentious intellectual property practice. He regularly advises on trade mark, copyright, database right, designs (registered and unregistered), passing off and domain name disputes involving clients in the television, sports, newspaper, retail and food and drink industries. Geoff acted on the widely reported Davidoff parallel importing case which was referred to the European Court of Justice and has particular expertise in grey market goods.

He also advises on sales promotion and advertising/copy clearance issues as well as brand strategy generally and managing trade mark portfolios.

Geoff is a member of The Intellectual Property Lawyers Organisation (TIPLO), an associate

member of the Institute of Trade Mark Agents
(ITMA) and sits on the Editorial Board of Trade-
mark World.

Macfarlanes is widely recognised as one of a
handful of high quality independent law firms in
the UK. With some 270 lawyers, the firm provides
a comprehensive service in its chosen areas of
expertise, handling work of a quality and scale
that places it among the leading law firms in
the City of London. The lawyers from each of
its four departments – Corporate, Private Client,
Litigation and Dispute Resolution, and Real Estate
– are consistently ranked among the leaders in
their field. Macfarlanes has a particularly strong
reputation in advising on intellectual property,
advertising, direct marketing, sales promotion
and PR issues – acting for a large number of major
brand owning clients.

Chapter

1

....

CREATING AND IDENTIFYING YOUR IP

Take away from English authors their copyrights, and you would very soon take away from England her authors.

Anthony Trollope, Autobiography

TRADE MARKS

What can you register as a trade mark?

Trade marks are essential tools for protecting the reputation and goodwill achieved by brands over their lifetime. They symbolise your quality and enable your customers to recognise your products or services quickly and effectively. If your trade mark is registered, you as proprietor have an exclusive right to use the mark for the goods or services for which it is registered for an initial period of 10 years, renewable upon payment of a fee for successive 10 year periods without limit. Once registered, you can rely on it to prevent a competitor from using an identical or similar mark. Registered trade marks are valuable property rights which can be licensed or assigned for considerable value. A portfolio of registered trade marks therefore adds significant value to your business. Trade mark registrations are granted on a 'first come first served' basis, so it is vital to make your application as soon as possible.

You should consider registering as a trade mark anything that is unique to your business and that is perceived by the public as a trade mark. It is not just your brand names and logos which can be registered as trade marks. Any sign which is capable of being represented graphically and of distinguishing your goods or services from those of other companies can be registered as a trade mark. Provided your mark has distinctive character and can distinguish the goods or services which it represents, you can in principle register any of the following categories as trade marks:

- company names
- brand names
- individuals' names
- words
- logos
- pictures
- letters
- numerals
- shapes
- packaging
- marketing slogans
- jingles
- music and other sounds
- domain names
- colours
- smells
- gestures

It is therefore possible to register non-traditional trade marks and you should be creative and think laterally when considering which marks to register. A word of warning though: the European Court of Justice has shown some reluctance to permit registrations for certain non-traditional trade marks. In the case of shape marks (e.g. bottles, electric shavers), in order for the shape to have the necessary distinctive character to be registered as a trade mark, consumers must rely upon the shape itself as an indication of trade origin when buying the goods: it is not enough that consumers recognise the shape, but rather consumers must, whenever they see the shape, think that the product originates from a particular manufacturer. In other words, the shape must be perceived by consumers as being a trade mark. In the case of smell, colour and sound marks, the description of the mark applied for must be self-contained, clear and precise.

There are three potential types of trade mark registration available to you, all of which will cover the UK: a UK registration; a European Community registration; and an international registration.

What can't you register as a trade mark?

Trade marks which are devoid of any distinctive character cannot be registered. For example, Macfarlanes could not register as a word mark 'GOOD ADVICE' for legal services because our competitors would no doubt claim that we are not alone in being able to provide good advice.

Purely descriptive marks cannot be registered as trade marks. This applies to marks that consist exclusively of signs or indications which would serve in trade to designate nothing more than the particulars of the goods or services themselves, e.g. 'BLOOD PRESSURE WATCH' for blood pressure meters, or again 'GOOD ADVICE' for legal services.

Trade marks consisting exclusively of signs or indications which have become generic descriptions in the relevant trade cannot be registered as trade marks, e.g. 'lino'.

There are further restrictions in respect of shape marks. A sign cannot be registered as a trade mark if it consists exclusively of (a) the shape which results from the nature of the goods themselves; (b) the shape of goods which is necessary to obtain a technical result; or (c) the shape which gives substantial value to the goods. For example, an application by Philips to register the shape of its three-dimensional rotary electric shavers was refused on the ground that the shape performed purely technical functions.

A trade mark will not be registered if it is contrary to public policy or to accepted principles of morality or if it is of such a nature as to deceive the public. For example, the mark 'www.standupifyouhatemanu.com' was rejected on the basis that it was antagonistic and could promote football violence.

Certain specially protected emblems cannot be registered as trade marks, e.g. the Union Jack, or representations of members of the royal family.

If a mark is applied for in bad faith, it will not be registrable. As a result, an application to register a trade mark must contain a statement that the mark is being used by the applicant or with its consent or that the applicant has a bona fide intention that the mark will be used. Applications made deliberately to block a competitor's use of a similar mark will not therefore be permitted.

Finally, a mark will not be registered if it conflicts with an earlier trade mark, i.e. it looks or sounds identical or similar to one already registered or applied for in respect of identical/similar goods or services.

Always conduct pre-emptive searches

In order to ensure that your mark is registrable and that it does not conflict with other existing registered marks, it is important at the outset, before embarking upon a new marketing initiative or product launch, to conduct a clearance search to ensure that you will be free to use the name or mark in question. Solicitors and/or trade mark agents should always be instructed, at the outset of a new advertising campaign, product launch or re-branding exercise, to conduct a trade mark search in respect of the word or mark that you want to use, before you start incurring any marketing costs and before you make any trade mark applications. This should be done as early as possible because you do not want to discover too late, via court proceedings, that a new campaign or new product name infringes an existing registered trade mark.

Registered trade mark searches can usually be conducted quickly and cheaply, within 24 hours if necessary, although naturally it is advisable to leave far more time if you want extensive and thorough searches to be undertaken in multiple jurisdictions. A search can be done for registrations of and pending applications for identical or similar trade marks in the UK or across Europe, or in any other jurisdiction where you will be using your mark. Unfortunately, there is no single database to search to clear a mark internationally and instead registered trade mark searches outside Europe are generally done on a jurisdiction by jurisdiction basis.

There are a number of trade marks searches available as follows:

- Quick and cheap online searches: this is a search that you can do yourself as a good starting point, but be aware that the results are not always accurate and comprehensive. Online searches of the UK Trade Marks Registry (see page 37) are available at www.patent.gov.uk; of the Community Trade Marks Registry (see page 44) at www.oami.eu.int; and of the WIPO database of Madrid Protocol registrations (see page 49) at www.wipo.int. You can search against particular words/text, proprietors or, if you know them, registration numbers.

- Registry searches: due to the limitations of online searches, it is often advisable in any event to instruct trade mark agents to conduct a comprehensive national search of the local trade mark registry. You will have to do this in countries where no online database is available (e.g. France and India).

- Specialist searches: for more comprehensive searches (e.g. to determine if there are any similar devices registered as trade marks), you will need to instruct trade mark agents or a specialist trade mark search agency such as Compu-Mark. You can limit your search to identical marks only or alternatively go for a 'full availability' search which also looks for confusingly similar marks. This will result in a clearance report which analyses all identical or similar marks worldwide if necessary. Thereafter, you should seek legal advice on the risks that any similar marks pose.

• A more extensive 'common law' search can be done to try to locate unregistered trade marks, involving searches of company registers, websites and trade press.

• Although clearance searches will give you considerable comfort, unfortunately no one can guarantee that you will not be sued or that you will definitely be successful in obtaining a trade mark registration. That said, trade mark searches are indispensable in assessing the risk of adopting a new mark.

Unregistered trade marks

The fact that you have not yet registered a particular trade mark does not mean that you have no protection. The law of passing off protects unregistered trade marks. In particular it protects reputation and goodwill by preventing third parties from using your name, get-up, unregistered trade mark, advertising theme or style, in such a way as to cause the public to be confused as to the origin of the third party's product or service.

In order to bring a passing off claim, you must establish that a third party has made a misrepresentation in the course of trade to a prospective customer or ultimate consumer, which is likely to injure your goodwill or business and which causes actual damage to you. Typically, passing off claims will be relevant to 'me too' look-alike products.

However, registering your mark as a trade mark provides wider protection than is available through the law of passing off and means that you can avoid the additional hurdles which have to be overcome in succeeding in a passing off claim. When a trade mark is registered, you will be granted a registration certificate which is proof of the ownership of the mark. In most cases you do not therefore need to prove goodwill or reputation, unlike the position under the law of passing off. Furthermore, if you as registered trade mark proprietor can show that a competitor is using an identical mark in respect of goods and/or services identical to your registration, you can prevent the use of the mark by that competitor without having to establish that the public has been confused by the competitor's use of the mark. As a result, suing for passing off tends to be more complex and therefore more expensive than suing for trade mark infringement, which is perhaps the most compelling reason to register your trade marks.

Use of ® and ™ symbols

You should always emphasise the status of a trade mark with the appropriate trade mark notice,

® or ™, and preferably also with a statement that the particular sign is a trade mark owned by your company. This allows you to assert your rights over the mark and alerts competitors in the market to the fact that you are the proprietor of that mark.

You should note, however, that the ® symbol or the abbreviation 'RTM', both of which designate a registered trade mark, can only be used by a registered trade mark owner. Use of the ® symbol or 'RTM' in conjunction with a mark that is not registered can constitute a criminal offence for falsely representing a trade mark as being registered.

A trade mark that has not been registered or that is incapable of registration can still, as I have explained, be protected from infringement under the law of passing off. In the case of unregistered trade marks, you cannot use the ® symbol but should instead use the ™ symbol to put the world on notice that the mark is an unregistered trade mark being used in a trade mark sense. The ™ symbol does not denote any specific protection other than that available under the law of passing off, but will hopefully cause people to think twice before infringing your unregistered trade mark and exposing themselves to a potential passing off claim.

COPYRIGHT
What is copyright all about?

The law of copyright rests on a very clear principle, namely that anyone who by his or her own skill and labour creates an original work shall, for a limited period, enjoy an exclusive right to copy that work.

You as a brand owner should hopefully already own the copyright in a myriad of works, such as your logos, labels, jingles, advertising, annual reports and brochures/catalogues, website content and possibly even slogans. Some of your works will themselves comprise a number of different types of copyright, for example your sales catalogue will contain both literary (the text) and artistic (the photographs/illustrations) works.

Unlike with trade marks, there is no cost involved in protecting copyright works because copyright protection arises automatically, as soon as the work has been created, and does not need to be registered. There is also no need to maintain a portfolio of your copyright works because copyright is not, like trade marks, renewable.

From a brand protection point of view, the most important thing for you to ensure is that, if you or your employees have not created the work in question, you have dealt adequately with the copyright ownership position. Is it important that you own the copyright? If so make sure that the creator assigns it to you. You don't want to find yourself in the same position as Dr Martens, who discovered that the copyright in their logo had been retained by a freelance designer who then assigned it to one of Dr Martens' competitors!

Why is copyright important? Because it gives you as owner of a copyright work the exclusive right to do certain acts which include copying the work, issuing copies of the work to the public, performing, showing or playing the work in public, or making an adaptation of the work. As owner of copyright in a work you can therefore stop someone else from doing those acts and in particular from copying the whole or a substantial part of your work.

What attracts copyright protection?

Copyright protection exists in the following categories of original works:

- literary works (e.g. books, articles, advertising scripts, computer programs, website content, brochures and, in certain cases, slogans and invented words)

- dramatic works (e.g. plays, works of dance or mime)
- musical works (e.g. melodies, jingles or theme tunes)
- artistic works (e.g. logos, labels, illustrations, photographs, paintings, drawings)
- films and broadcasts
- sound recordings
- typographical arrangements

What does not attract copyright protection?

Copyright protection does not cover works which are not original. Your work therefore needs to be original in the sense that it must not have been copied from other works; it does not, however, have to be 'novel' or unique. In order to obtain copyright protection you must have expended certain skill, labour and judgement in the creation of the work. However, there is no de minimis quality requirement: as long as your work is original, it will be entitled to copyright protection, regardless of its artistic merit.

Copyright does not subsist unless the work is recorded in a permanent form, for example in writing or in a sketch.

Protecting your ideas

Copyright does not protect general ideas. There can be no copyright in an idea which is merely in the head. Copyright does, however, protect the way in which an idea is expressed. Therefore, if ideas are sufficiently detailed and set out, for example, in a written synopsis, they can be protected by way of copyright.

If you believe the underlying concept or idea is valuable and unique, and you want to develop it further, you should not just rely on copyright protection. The concept should also be protected separately by way of a confidentiality agreement which you should enter into with anyone to whom your idea is disclosed.

Make sure that you own the copyright

The first owner of copyright in a work is generally the author of that work, i.e. the creator of it.

However, where the author or creator of the work is one of your employees, who creates the work in the course of his employment, you do not need to worry because you as employer will be the first owner of the copyright in the work.

In respect of non-employees, there are specific rules relating to more unusual copyright works. For example, the first owner of copyright in:

- sound recordings is the producer of the sound recordings and not the musicians
- a film is the producer and the principal director jointly
- a broadcast is the person who makes the broadcast
- a cable programme is the person providing the cable programme service in which the programme is included
- typographical arrangements of published editions is the publisher

Where you commission works to be created by third parties it is of critical importance that you agree at the outset who will own the copyright. The starting point is that copyright will be owned by the third party creator. If this is not what you want, then you need to deal with the position contractually. Do you need to own the copyright? If so, you will need an assignment from the creator. Alternatively, will you be happy to take a licence of the copyright, and if so on an exclusive or non-exclusive basis? For a further explanation of licences and assignments and the differences between them, see page 102.

Some examples of cases where you as brand owner will use third parties but may want them to assign copyright in their work to you are as follows:

- Advertising agencies: you will want to own the copyright in the advertising copy that they produce.
- Branding consultants: if you re-brand and retain consultants to devise a new logo/corporate image for you, presumably you will want to own the rights in it.
- Website designers: again, you will want them to assign copyright in the artwork and layout of your website to you.
- Freelance copywriters: if you appoint a freelance writer to prepare the narrative for your annual report or sales catalogue/brochure, you should ensure that he assigns copyright in his literary work to you. Similarly, you may want to own the artistic copyright in any photographs that you have commissioned.

It is very important to keep on top of your ownership of copyright. If it is not properly assigned and you do not keep track of which entity owns the particular copyright, this can lead to difficulties when enforcement action is required as you must establish first that you own the copyright. When was the last time that you reviewed who owns the copyright in your logos, labels or packaging designs?

Period of copyright protection

Copyright in a work does not last forever and is not renewable. The period of protection depends upon the type of work.

For literary, dramatic, musical and artistic works, the term of protection is the life of the author plus 70 years. Copyright in films lasts for 70 years from the death of the last to survive of the principal director, the author of the screenplay, the author of the dialogue and the composer of music created specifically for and used in the film.

Copyright in a sound recording lasts for 50 years from the end of the year in which it was made. However, if it is was released within that time, copyright lasts for 50 years from the end of the year of release.

Copyright in broadcasts expires 50 years after the end of the calendar year in which the broadcast was made.

Copyright in cable programmes expires 50 years after the end of the calendar year in which it was included in a cable programme service.

Copyright in published editions expires 25 years after the end of the calendar year in which the edition was first published.

Moral rights

There are two key moral rights automatically available to the creator of a copyright work:

- The right of 'paternity': the author of a literary, dramatic, musical or artistic work has the right to be identified as the author.
- The right of 'integrity': such authors also have the right to object to any derogatory treatment of their work, such as additions, deletions or adaptations.

One other thing to look out for when commissioning copyright works to be created for you by a third party is moral rights. If you want an assignment of the copyright to you, you will probably also want the creator to waive his moral rights (copyright law does not permit moral rights to be assigned as they are, by their nature, personal to the creator).

If, for example, you retain a freelance writer to prepare your sales brochure, you may not want to have to credit him with writing the narrative. You therefore need to ensure, in the contract of appointment, that he agrees to waive his moral rights.

Your employees who produce works in the course of their employment are not entitled to moral rights.

Moral rights last for as long as the copyright term of protection.

DATABASE RIGHT
What is database right?

You may not appreciate it, but you are probably already the owner of database right in a number of your databases (e.g. customer contact details, mailing lists, market surveys, your well-ordered trade mark portfolio). Database right is a European right introduced in 1997 but is likely to be less relevant to you as a brand owner than trade marks, copyright and designs. What follows is therefore only a brief overview of this evolving IP right.

Database right was created because in some countries the requirement that copyright works be original was such that, although databases were expensive to create and valuable to exploit, they were mere arrangements of information and did not always qualify for copyright protection.

So the new right covers:

• databases: which is any collection of independent works, data or other materials which are (a) arranged in a systematic or methodical way, and (b) individually accessible by electronic or other (e.g. a paper database) means;

- in which there has been a substantial investment: in order to have database right protection, you must have invested in obtaining, verifying or presenting the contents of the database, as opposed to any investment in *creating* the underlying information.

As with copyright, there is no cost involved in protecting your databases. Database right arises automatically upon creation of the database and there is no registration system.

What protection does database right give you?

If your database does qualify for database right, the protection you receive is broader than under copyright law which always requires some form of copying.

Database right on the other hand is infringed where a person:

- extracts or reutilises (note the absence of the word 'copies') all or a *substantial* part of your database; or
- repeatedly and systematically extracts or reutilises *insubstantial* parts of your database.

Database right is not infringed by fair dealing in a database which has been made available to the public.

Database right lasts for 15 years from the end of the calendar year in which the database was made. Database right is not renewable, but databases of course tend to be constantly evolving and in that respect your database will be protected for perpetuity because each time you amend it the 15 year period arguably starts again.

In what respect do you need to bother with database right for the purposes of your brand strategy?

Make sure you own the database right:

- The first owner of database right is the person who takes the initiative in obtaining, verifying or presenting the contents of the database and who assumes the risk of investing in it.
- In practice, this means that commissioning the creation of a database should be less problematic than in the case of copyright works because you as commissioner will have invested in the preparation of the database and should therefore be the first owner.

- Nonetheless, it is prudent to ensure that, in the terms of appointment, any third party commissioned to do any form of creative work for you assigns all IP rights to you including database right.
- As with copyright, where one of your employees makes the database in the course of his employment, you as employer will automatically own any database right.

Don't forget about it: database right might provide a more obscure claim for you against infringers. For example, where you suspect that a competitor is using your mailing list but you have no evidence of copying, database right infringement may be a more straightforward claim.

Trojan horses: an old (but important) trick of the trade is to include some bogus or meaningless data in your database to prove, beyond doubt, that someone else has had access to and utilised, extracted or copied it. For example, in a customer list you could include the maiden name of a director's wife.

DESIGNS

Designs is an area often overlooked by brand owners, not least because design law is a complex area of intellectual property law. Somewhat confusingly, there are four different forms of design protection available, each of which has arbitrary differences: UK registered designs; UK unregistered designs (often referred to merely as design right); registered European Community designs; and unregistered European Community designs.

As a brand owner, you need to be aware of what can be registered as a design. For example, it is possible to register not only your products but also your logo and packaging as a UK and/or community design.

Whenever a new product is devised, you should therefore consider whether to register its design.

Before launching a new product design, you should also, at an early stage in the product's creation, instruct patent attorneys or external counsel to check that there are no similar designs or patents already registered. This is important for two reasons. First, you do not want your new product to infringe someone else's rights. Second, you want to ensure that your design is original enough to be registered.

UK registered designs

These cover your two- and three-dimensional product designs, including the product itself, its packaging and get-up. The definition of a 'product' is sufficiently wide to include your logos and graphic symbols.

The appearance of the whole or a part of a product can be registered as a design at the UK Patent Office, if the appearance results from features such as the lines, contours, colours, shape, texture or materials of the product or its ornamentation.

As with copyright, your design does not need to have any aesthetic merit or 'eye appeal' to be registrable. It does, however, have to satisfy both of the following two tests:

- *Novelty*: your design must be new and must not have been disclosed anywhere in the world before you apply for the registration. So if you have devised a new product design, do not use it in trade or exhibit it at trade shows until you have applied to have it registered. (Although there is actually a 12-month grace period to allow a designer to market a design or seek financial backing, you should exercise caution and apply to register your design as soon as possible without disclosing it.)
- *Individual character*: the overall impression of your design must differ from the overall impression of any earlier publicly available design, as judged through the eyes of an 'informed user'.

Certain features of your product cannot be registered as designs, e.g. features whose shape/design is dictated solely by the product's 'technical function' or by the need to form part of or attach to another product (often referred to as the 'must fit' and 'must match' exclusions). For example, a camera film cartridge has to be a specific size and shape to fit into the camera casing so that element of the film cartridge will not be registrable as a design.

The first term of protection for a UK registered design is five years, but it can be renewed, on payment of a fee, up to four times, giving a maximum of 25 years' protection.

The person who can apply to register a design is the author/creator of the design, save for two exceptions of importance to you:

• Commissioned designs: unlike with copyright (see page 15), you need not worry about obtaining an assignment from any third party creator. If you commission a third party to design a product for you, you as the commissioner will be the first owner of the rights in the design and you can apply to register it.
• Employees: as with copyright, you as employer will be the first owner of the rights in a design created by your employees in the course of their employment.

UK unregistered designs

The fact that you have not registered your product as a design does not mean that you have no rights in it. UK law recognises unregistered designs (also known as 'design right') in certain three-dimensional articles, although this will not cover logos which are two dimensional.

Confusingly, the test for which designs qualify for design right is different to the test for registered designs. In order to qualify for design right protection, your design must:

- *be original and not commonplace*: it must not have copied another design (which is different to the novelty test for registered designs); and it must not be commonplace in the design field in question at the time of its creation; and
- *relate to any aspect of the shape or configuration of the whole or part of an article*: the key point here is that design right does not subsist in mere surface decoration. So if you design an original shape and pattern for a cup, the shape of the cup will attract design right, but the pattern will not (although it may be an artistic work and therefore protected by copyright). Similarly, design right does not cover logos.

As with registered designs, features that are necessary for their technical function or to fit/match another product do not attract design right.

The period of protection for unregistered design right is either:

- 10 years from first sale; or
- 15 years from design/manufacture if it is not put on sale.

As with registered designs, if you commission a design from a third party, or if your employee creates the design in the course of his employment, you will automatically own the design right without the need for an assignment.

European Community designs (registered and unregistered)

These cover your two- and three-dimensional product designs. It is worth reviewing your trade mark and product portfolio to establish whether there are any post-March 2002 designs that you may now want to register as community designs. Going forward, you should always consider whether new logos or product designs should be registered as community designs as well as trade marks.

By way of example, some designs that have been registered as community designs include diaries, chairs, vases, shoes, circular saws and toothbrushes.

Since March 2002 the EU has added a community-wide protection to the various national protections that already existed for designs. There is now an automatic three-year protection for 'unregistered community designs' and up to a maximum of 25 years' protection for 'registered community designs'.

These new rights protect the design of a product; both concepts are broadly defined:

- A *design* is the appearance of the whole or part of a product resulting from its lines, contours, colours, shape, texture and/or materials and/or ornamentation.
- A *product* is any industrial or handicraft item, including packaging, graphic symbols/logos and fonts, but excluding computer programs.

This means that community design rights do not protect only those items which would usually be thought of as consumer designs – e.g. mobile phones, irons, staplers – but can also cover your logos and packaging/shapes.

As with UK registered designs, any design which is *novel* and has *individual character* qualifies for community design protection. This means that there must have been no previous identical design and your design must give users a different overall impression so that they can tell it apart from other designs.

The first owner of community design right will be the designer or, if he is an employee, his employer. Unlike with UK registered or unregistered designs, the commissioner of a design will not be the first owner of any community design right. Therefore, as with copyright, if you retain a third party to create a design for you, you need to ensure that you have dealt adequately with the community design ownership position and ideally you will get the designer to assign his community design right to you.

Unregistered community design right takes effect immediately when you make the design available to the public and allows you to prevent it from being copied within the EU. However, it lasts for only three years if not registered. If you register a design within a year of making it available to the public (note that after that year the design will no longer be seen as 'new' and will not therefore be registrable), you will have a monopoly in that design in the EU. You can then prevent anyone making a product to that design, whether or not they copied your design to do so, for up to 25 years. Unlike trade marks, registered designs cannot be renewed beyond the maximum 25 years' protection. Registration is nonetheless beneficial as it provides wider protection against independent development of the same or a similar design without you necessarily having to prove copying.

The first term of protection for a community registered design is five years but it can be renewed, on payment of a fee, up to four times, giving a total of 25 years' protection.

There are limits to what can be protected. As with UK registered designs, where a product looks the way it does simply because it needs that appearance in order to perform its function (for example, a wheel has to be round), that element of the design will not be protected. The same applies to those elements of the design which are needed to allow one product to be connected to another, such as plugs and other connections (the 'must fit' and 'must match' exclusions).

Overlap between trade marks and designs

Your device marks and logos which are applied to your products will constitute designs for the purposes of UK registered designs and community registered and unregistered designs, as they relate to the appearance of a product.

As long as your device marks and logos are new and have individual character, they can be registered as designs as well as trade marks.

Benefits of registering device marks/logos as designs

You will need to consider this on a case by case basis and seek advice as to the necessity and cost effectiveness of registering your device marks/ logos as both trade marks and designs, but here are some benefits:

- The design registration process (both UK and community) is quicker and cheaper than the trade mark registration system.
- Unlike trade mark registrations, a design registration does not only protect you in relation to limited classes of goods. Trade marks do not give monopoly rights, whereas registered designs can give you up to 25 years' monopoly protection during which no one else can use your design in respect of any goods without your permission.
- If your trade mark is not distinctive enough, or is descriptive, it will not be registered as a trade mark, but this does not prevent it from being registered as a design. Similarly, unlike with registered trade marks, there is no risk that the way in which you use your logo will result in

the revocation of your design registration where the brand's distinctiveness is diminished, e.g. where it is being used as a decorative motif resulting in the consumer no longer associating the product with the brand owner.

• Unlike with trade marks, your design registration is not capable of being revoked for non-use.

Chapter

2

....

REGISTERING
YOUR IP

Property has its duties as well as its rights.
                                        Thomas Drummond

TRADE MARKS
The Nice classification system

Trade marks are registrable by reference to defined classes of the goods and services upon which you use or intend to use them.

The Nice Agreement provides for an internationally recognised standard classification of goods and services – 34 classes of goods and 11 classes of services – for which trade marks are registrable (see page 52). However, a single application for a trade mark in a number of classes can be made (subject to an additional fee per class).

The general nature of many of the classifications may mean that you wish to specify the type of goods and services you are using the mark for; first, to list exhaustively the type of goods and services in connection with which you will be using the mark (for the purposes of trade mark oppositions or infringement actions); and second, to carve out certain goods and services to avoid your registrations within a class being open to challenge on the basis of non-use. It is important to give careful consideration to the classes of goods and services that you want to register as your application will define your future rights to bring infringement proceedings against third party infringers.

It is possible to divide and share registrations within the same class. For example, the Automobile Association and American Airlines both have UK trade mark registrations for the mark 'AA' in Class 39 which covers 'transport; packaging and storage of goods; travel arrangements'. The Automobile Association registration specifically covers 'recovery and inspection of vehicles and vehicle towing systems' while American Airlines' registration covers 'air transportation of passengers and freight'.

A registered trade mark covering the UK can be obtained in one or more of three ways: a UK registration; a European Community registration; or an international registration. I will now consider each in turn.

UK registrations

The application procedure

An application to register a trade mark in the UK is made to the UK Trade Marks Registry, which is part of the Patent Office, for a fixed fee for a mark in one class and an additional fee for each further class. Before making any application you should conduct a pre-emptive search (see page 6). The application is made on a standard application form (Form TM3) or electronically.

Once you have made your application, a Trade Marks Registry examiner will review it and send you an examination report (normally within two months of the Registry receiving your application). This report will tell you if your mark is acceptable. The examiner can object to your mark on 'absolute grounds' (e.g. if the mark is purely descriptive, has become customary in that particular line of trade, is offensive, or is not distinctive) or on 'relative grounds'. Relative grounds apply where someone else has got there first; for example, where your mark is, in relation to a mark which somebody else has already registered or applied to register:

- identical in connection with identical goods or services
- identical in connection with similar goods or services or similar in connection with identical or similar goods or services, where there is also a likelihood of confusion on the part of the public

In addition, although the examiner will only examine an application against prior trade marks in relevant classes on the UK and CTM registers, relative grounds can also exist where your mark conflicts with an earlier copyright work or design or an unregistered trade mark, or where a mark is identical or similar to a well-known mark in respect of any goods or services, where your mark would take unfair advantage of or be detrimental to the distinctive character or repute of that well-known mark.

However, the examination procedure for the UK Trade Marks Registry is currently in a state of flux. The current system of the examiner making official objections to a mark on 'relative grounds' is inconsistent with the Community trade mark regime and will soon be abolished. Instead, the Registry examiner will still conduct an official search for conflicting earlier marks but this will only be used for information purposes. If the Registry examiner finds a relevant prior application or registration, both the applicant and the earlier mark's owner will be informed of the potential conflict, although the Registry will accept and publish the application as filed. It will then be up to the applicant to withdraw or restrict his application to avoid conflict, or up to the earlier mark's owner to oppose the later application or to attack the resulting registration. The new Registry regime is likely to come into force in October 2007.

If the examiner raises an official objection, whether on absolute grounds or (until October 2007) on relative grounds, you will then have up to six months to try to persuade the Registry that the objections are not justified and to overcome them. You can telephone or write to the examiner. If there are relatively straightforward ways of overcoming the Registry's objections, for example by amending the description of the classes in which it is proposed to be registered, the examiner will tell you about these in the examination report.

You can also apply to have a formal meeting with a hearing officer, who is a senior official in the Trade Marks Registry. This will give you the opportunity to put forward your case, which will allow the hearing officer to make a decision on the future of your application. If you cannot overcome the objections you can either withdraw your application or the Registry will write to you telling you that it has been refused. You can, however, appeal against the Registry's decision (see page 43).

Hopefully your mark will be accepted by the Registry, in which case the next step is that it will be advertised in the *Trade Marks Journal* which is published every Friday. Following this advertisement, there is a period of three months which allows anyone else (e.g. your competitors or third parties with similar marks to your application) to oppose the registration of your mark. The Registry will write and tell you if anybody does oppose your mark and you will then need to decide whether you want to contest the opposition, withdraw your application or negotiate a coexistence agreement.

The length of the process of registering a trade mark obviously depends on whether the Registry or a third party objects to your application but, subject to it not encountering any obstacles, it normally takes around six months for a trade mark to become registered.

Opposing third parties' trade mark applications

You can oppose a UK application on absolute or relative grounds, as discussed on page 38.

To oppose a UK application, you should tell the applicant in writing why you are thinking of opposing their application. You can get their address from the *Trade Marks Journal* in which their application was advertised. If you cannot resolve the issue informally, you should send a 'Notice of Opposition and Statement of Grounds' (Form TM7) to the Trade Marks Registry (with a fixed fee) within three months of the advertisement of the application. This time limit cannot be extended.

The Registry then sends the Notice of Opposition to the applicant, who has three months to send back a 'Notice of Defence and Counterstatement' (Form TM8). It is worth noting that the party which loses the opposition proceedings usually has to contribute to the other side's costs. Either

side can ask for a 'cooling off' period of 12 months
from the Notice of Opposition. This will only be
implemented if both parties agree to it, to try to
negotiate a resolution.

As the opponent you have three months to file
your evidence, and the applicant then has a further
three months to file his. Finally, you then have a
further three months to file evidence in reply.
There may then be a hearing, following which the
Registry will send you its decision within about
four to six weeks. This decision is subject to
appeal (see page 43).

In advance of the evidential stage, for an opposition based upon conflicting trade mark registrations or applications for identical or similar
goods or services, the Registry will send both
sides a 'preliminary indication' setting out what
it thinks the likely outcome of the opposition
proceedings will be. The preliminary indication
has no legal status, but naturally may dissuade a
party from proceeding any further. If either side
does not agree with the preliminary indication
and wants to pursue the matter further, they can
send the Registry a 'Request to Proceed to the
Evidential Rounds' (Form TM53).

Registration

Assuming there is no opposition to your mark or
that any opposition is unsuccessful, your mark

will then be registered and you will be sent a registration certificate by the Registry. Your registration will last for 10 years, following which you may renew your registration on payment of a fixed renewal fee per class for successive periods of 10 years.

However, if you do not use the trade mark in the UK on the goods or services for which it is registered in the five years from the registration of the mark or for any subsequent continuous period of five years, and if there are no proper reasons why the trade mark has not been used, another party may apply to revoke your trade mark registration. The earliest time such a revocation application can occur is therefore five years after the registration of the mark.

A UK registration does not protect your trade mark abroad. If you use your mark in other countries, you can protect it by obtaining a community or international registration (see pages 44 and 49).

Appeals

All decisions of the Trade Marks Registry, excluding those on classification and whether a matter in an application should be treated as confidential, are subject to appeal.

You can choose whether to appeal to the High Court or to an 'Appointed Person' who is a barrister, senior solicitor or judge appointed by the Lord Chancellor and who sits as part of the Trade Mark Registry.

Appealing to the Appointed Person is cheaper. There is no fee and costs are similar to those of a Registry hearing. However, an appeal to the Appointed Person carries with it no further appeal, either by leave or by right, and can only be challenged in very limited circumstances by judicial review.

An appeal to the High Court carries a fixed fee and higher costs, including hourly court fees. However, the court's decision may, with leave, be further appealed to the Court of Appeal.

Appeals of a decision of the Registry must be made within 28 days of the date of that decision, by written notice to the Registrar in the case of an appeal to the Appointed Person or by filing an Appellant's Notice at the Chancery Division in the case of an appeal to the High Court.

Community registrations

The application procedure

In addition to or instead of a UK application, you can also apply for a community trade mark (CTM) which enables you to obtain a single registration throughout the EC. CTM applications are administered by the Office for Harmonisation in the Internal Market (OHIM) in Alicante, Spain.

An application for a CTM registration must be made in writing and can be made in any of the official languages of the EC (not just the five OHIM languages of Spanish, German, English, French and Italian), although one of those five official languages must be designated as a second language. The application must be made on an official OHIM form which can be obtained from OHIM or the Patent Office. This should be filed directly at OHIM, via the Patent Office, or electronically. The Patent Office charges a handling fee for an OHIM application. There is a fixed fee for CTM applications in up to three classes plus a further fee for each additional class. Another fee for the first three classes plus a class fee for each additional class must also be paid upon registration.

Upon receiving an application, OHIM will issue a filing receipt and then examine the application for formalities, for specification and classification issues and then upon absolute grounds, which broadly mirror those under the UK system explained on page 38. If there are objections, OHIM will write to inform you and you generally have two months to respond.

Unlike in the UK, no relative grounds examination is made by the OHIM examiner. However, OHIM checks its own register for earlier marks, and also sends a copy of the application to the Trade Mark Offices of the EC Member States which have agreed to check their national registers against the CTM application. Not all states have agreed to do so, for example France, Italy and Germany do not. A report of the checks is then sent to the applicant, for his information. However, OHIM will not itself raise a relative grounds objection to the application, leaving any conflict to be resolved through opposition or through a post-registration invalidity action.

Once the application has been accepted by OHIM, it is published in the CTM Bulletin for a three-month opposition period and if no oppositions are lodged, OHIM invites the applicant to pay the registration fee.

Oppositions

Anyone wishing to oppose your application must do so within three months of publication of the application. The CTM application can only be opposed on the relative grounds for refusal, which broadly mirror those under the UK system explained on page 38. Objections on absolute grounds can be raised by a third party only through filing informal observations, or through filing an invalidity action after registration.

If your application is opposed, you as applicant are then given a 'cooling off' period of two months within which to withdraw or limit your application before opposition proceedings formally commence. The 'cooling off' period can be extended by a further 22 months if both parties jointly request it. OHIM oppositions are decided on the basis of written arguments, without an oral hearing. The opponent's evidence must be filed within two months of the commencement of proceedings and you as applicant must file your observations within a further two months of this date. The opponent then has two months to reply, following which a decision will be made by OHIM.

If your CTM application is withdrawn or refused, in many circumstances you may nonetheless convert it into a national application in one or more Member States. An application for conversion must be made to OHIM within three months of the refusal at community level.

Registration

Assuming no opposition has been filed or that the opposition has been decided in your favour, your mark will be recorded in the Register of CTMs following payment of the registration fee.

A CTM registration lasts for 10 years from the date of the filing of the application and can thereafter be renewed for successive periods of 10 years.

It should be noted that a CTM can be revoked, on the application of a third party, for non-use if it has not been used anywhere in the EC for a continuous period of five years, unless there are proper reasons for this non-use. However, it is not necessary for the mark to be used in every single Member State of the EC.

Appeals

You can appeal an adverse OHIM decision to the Board of Appeal. A notice of appeal must be filed at OHIM, together with the fixed appeal fee, within two months of the date of the decision and a written statement setting out the grounds of appeal must be filed within four months. If there are fundamental deficiencies in OHIM's decision, the Board may set aside the decision and remit the case to OHIM for reconsideration or decide the matter itself.

You can also appeal an adverse decision of the Board of Appeal to the European Court of Justice (ECJ) on the grounds of lack of competence, infringement of an essential procedural requirement, infringement of EC law or misuse of power. These grounds are so broad that they cover most instances in which a party claims the Board of Appeal's decision is wrong. An appeal to the ECJ is brought by filing a notice of appeal within two months of notification of the decision of the Board of Appeal.

International registrations

You can also apply for an international trade mark registration by one central application through what is known as the Madrid System. The registration is effective in all countries which are signatories of the Madrid Protocol. This includes the UK, most of the European Union, the USA, China and Korea. In order to apply for international registration of a mark you must have an existing application or registration of the trade mark in your country of origin.

An application for international registration may be made by any national in a contracting state or any other person who lives in or has an industrial or commercial establishment in a contracting state. The application must designate in which countries you wish the trade mark to be effective.

An international application must be filed with the office of origin (in the UK, the Trade Mark Registry) who will then transmit it to the International Bureau of the World International Property Organisation (WIPO) in Geneva. The application must be in the prescribed form (in the UK, Form MM2) and be accompanied by a

handling fee sheet and a fixed handling fee
payable to the Trade Marks Registry. The application fee consists of a basic fee in Swiss francs
plus a designation fee and a supplementary fee
for each class of goods and services beyond the
third.

WIPO will examine the application to check that
it meets the formalities and will then register the
mark and send a certificate to the holder. It must
then notify the offices of the designated contracting states of the international registration without
delay and inform the office of origin. The registration is then published in the *Gazette of International Marks*. The date of the registration will
normally be the date on which the office of origin
received the international application provided
that the International Bureau receives it within
two months of this date.

An international registration which designates
the UK is examined for absolute and relative
grounds for refusal as explained on page 38 and,
if accepted by the Registrar, is advertised in the
Trade Marks Journal and is then open to opposition by third parties in the normal way. This
will be true of other contracting party states,
albeit subject to differences in their national
legislation and procedure.

If there has been no third party opposition, the
mark will then become a protected international

trade mark within the UK following expiry of the opposition period.

The protection of an international registration can be extended to further contracting parties by making a subsequent designation.

From the date of international registration, each designated contracting state must afford the mark the same protection as if it had been filed directly in the office of that contracting state. Each designated contracting state has the right to refuse protection to an international registration in its territory on the grounds that it would have been refused under the legislation of that contracting state if the mark had been filed directly with the office of that contracting state.

A major disadvantage of the Madrid System is that of central attack. This means that an international registration will cease to be effective in all the states in which it had effect if the basic application is withdrawn or limited or is the subject of a final decision of rejection, revocation, cancellation or invalidation within five years from its registration.

An international registration lasts initially for 10 years and can be renewed for successive 10-year periods thereafter.

Separate and distinct from international registrations under the Madrid Protocol, it is of course open to you to apply for national trade mark registrations in specific countries of importance to you. I have detailed the procedure for UK applications at pages 37–44 but for other countries local advice should be sought.

The standard Nice classification of goods and services for trade mark registrations (from 1 January 2007)

(Crown Copyright reproduced with the kind permission of the Patent Office)

Goods

Class 1

Chemicals used in industry, science and photography, as well as in agriculture, horticulture and forestry; unprocessed artificial resins, unprocessed plastics; manures; fire extinguishing compositions; tempering and soldering preparations; chemical substances for preserving foodstuffs; tanning substances; adhesives used in industry.

Includes chemicals for the making of products belonging to other classes.

Does not include fungicides, herbicides, insecticides or preparations for destroying vermin which are in Class 5.

Class 2

Paints, varnishes, lacquers; preservatives against rust and against deterioration of wood; colourants; mordants; raw natural resins; metals in foil and powder form for painters, decorators, printers and artists.

Does not include paint boxes for children which are in Class 16 or insulating paints and varnishes which are in Class 17.

Class 3

Bleaching preparations and other substances for laundry use; cleaning, polishing, scouring and abrasive preparations; soaps; perfumery, essential oils, cosmetics, hair lotions; dentifrices.

Includes deodorants for personal use.

Does not include scented candles which are in Class 4 or air deodorising preparations which are in Class 5.

Class 4

Industrial oils and greases; lubricants; dust absorbing, wetting and binding compositions; fuels (including motor spirit) and illuminants; candles and wicks for lighting.

Includes combustible fuels and scented candles.

Does not include fuel for nuclear reactors or electricity which are both in Class 1.

Class 5

Pharmaceutical and veterinary preparations; sanitary preparations for medical purposes; dietetic substances adapted for medical use, food for babies; plasters, materials for dressings; material for stopping teeth, dental wax; disinfectants; preparations for destroying vermin; fungicides, herbicides.

Includes foods and beverages which are adapted for medical purposes.

Does not include supportive bandages which are in Class 10.

Class 6

Common metals and their alloys; metal building materials; transportable buildings of metal; materials of metal for railway tracks; non-electric cables and wires of common metal; ironmongery, small items of metal hardware; pipes and tubes of metal; safes; goods of common metal not included in other classes; ores.

Includes unwrought and partly wrought common metals as well as simple products made of them;

metallic windows and doors and also metallic framed conservatories.

Class 7

Machines and machine tools; motors and engines (except for land vehicles); machine coupling and transmission components (except for land vehicles); agricultural implements other than hand-operated; incubators for eggs.

Includes parts of engines and motors; some parts for vehicles (e.g. exhausts for vehicles); vacuum cleaners.

Does not include engines or motors for land vehicles which are in Class 12 or specialist machines (e.g. weighing machines are in Class 9).

Class 8

Hand tools and implements (hand operated); cutlery; side-arms; razors.

Includes electric razors and hair cutters; cutlery made of precious metal.

Does not include surgical cutlery which is in Class 10 or hand held and electrically powered tools (e.g. electric drills are in Class 7).

Class 9

Scientific, nautical, surveying, photographic, cinematographic, optical, weighing, measuring, signalling, checking (supervision), life-saving and teaching apparatus and instruments; apparatus and instruments for conducting, switching, transforming, accumulating, regulating or controlling electricity; apparatus for recording, transmission or reproduction of sound or images; magnetic data carriers, recording discs; automatic vending machines and mechanisms for coin operated apparatus; cash registers; calculating machines, data processing equipment and computers; fire-extinguishing apparatus.

Includes computer hardware and firmware; computer software (including software downloadable from the Internet); compact discs; digital music (downloadable from the Internet); telecommunications apparatus; computer games equipment adapted for use with TV receivers; mouse mats; mobile phone accessories; contact lenses, spectacles and sunglasses; clothing for protection against accident, irradiation or fire.

Does not include printed computer manuals which are in Class 16, self-contained computer games equipment which is in Class 28, various electrical items (e.g. electric screwdrivers are in Class 7 and electric toothbrushes are in Class 21).

Class 10

Surgical, medical, dental and veterinary apparatus and instruments, artificial limbs, eyes and teeth; orthopaedic articles; suture materials.

Includes electro-medical or surgical apparatus; massage apparatus.

Does not include contact lenses, spectacles or sunglasses which are in Class 9 or wheelchairs which are in Class 12.

Class 11

Apparatus for lighting, heating, steam generating, cooking, refrigerating, drying, ventilating, water supply and sanitary purposes.

Includes air conditioning apparatus; electric kettles; gas and electric cookers; vehicle lights.

Class 12

Vehicles; apparatus for locomotion by land, air or water.

Includes motors and engines for land vehicles and certain other parts and fittings (e.g. vehicle body parts and transmissions).

Does not include certain parts or fittings for vehicles (e.g. exhausts and starters are in Class 7, lights and air conditioning units are in Class 11) or children's toy bicycles which are in Class 28.

Class 13

Firearms; ammunition and projectiles, explosives; fireworks.

Does not include apparatus for use in playing paintball combat games which are in Class 28.

Class 14

Precious metals and their alloys and goods in precious metals or coated therewith, not included in other classes; jewellery, precious stones; horological and chronometric instruments.

Includes clocks and watches; costume jewellery.

Does not include certain precious metal items (e.g. cutlery is in Class 8, pens are in Class 16).

Class 15

Musical instruments.

Includes stands and cases adapted for musical instruments.

Class 16

Paper, cardboard and goods made from these materials, not included in other classes; printed matter; bookbinding material; photographs; stationery; adhesives for stationery or household purposes; artists' materials; paint brushes; typewriters and office requisites (except furniture); instructional and teaching material (except apparatus); plastic materials for packaging (not included in other classes); printers' type; printing blocks.

Includes disposable nappies of paper for babies; printed publications.

Does not include adhesives for industrial purposes which are in Class 1, electronic publications (downloadable) which are in Class 9, providing electronic publications (not downloadable) which are in Class 41 or wallpaper which is in Class 27.

Class 17

Rubber, gutta-percha, gum, asbestos, mica and goods made from these materials and not included in other classes; plastics in extruded form for use in manufacture; packing, stopping and insulating materials; flexible pipes, not of metal.

Includes semi-finished plastics materials for use in further manufacture.

Does not include unprocessed plastics in the form of liquids, chips, granules etc. which are in Class 1.

Class 18

Leather and imitations of leather, and goods made of these materials and not included in other classes; animal skins, hides; trunks and travelling bags; umbrellas, parasols and walking sticks; whips, harnesses and saddlery.

Includes handbags, rucksacks, purses; clothing for animals.

Does not include leather clothing which is in Class 9 (for protection against injury) or in Class 25 (ordinary apparel); certain specialist leather articles (e.g. cheque book holders are in Class 16).

Class 19

Building materials (non-metallic); non-metallic rigid pipes for building; asphalt, pitch and bitumen; non-metallic transportable buildings; monuments, not of metal.

Includes non-metallic framed conservatories, doors and windows.

Class 20

Furniture, mirrors, picture frames; goods (not included in other classes) of wood, cork, reed, cane, wicker, horn, bone, ivory, whalebone, shell, amber, mother-of-pearl, meerschaum and substitutes for all these materials, or of plastics.

Includes both metallic and non-metallic furniture including garden furniture; pillows and cushions.

Does not include furniture adapted for laboratory use which is in Class 9, furniture adapted for medical use which is in Class 10 or duvets or covers for pillows, cushions or duvets which are in Class 24.

Class 21

Household or kitchen utensils and containers (not of precious metal or coated therewith); combs and sponges; brushes (except paint brushes); brush-making materials; articles for cleaning purposes; steel wool; unworked or semi-worked glass (except glass used in building); glassware, porcelain and earthenware not included in other classes.

Includes both electric and non-electric toothbrushes.

Does not include electric kitchen appliances (e.g. electric food processors are in Class 7, electric kettles are in Class 11) or kitchen and table cutlery which is in Class 8.

Class 22

Ropes, string, nets, tents, awnings, tarpaulins, sails, sacks and bags (not included in other classes); padding and stuffing materials (except of rubber or plastics); raw fibrous textile materials.

Includes bags and sacks for transporting bulk materials.

Class 23

Yarns and threads, for textile use.

Class 24

Textiles and textile goods, not included in other classes; bed and table covers.

Includes textile piece goods; textiles for making articles of clothing.

Does not include electric blankets (not for medical use) which are in Class 11 or table linen which is in Class 16.

Class 25

Clothing, footwear, headgear.

Does not include clothing for the prevention of accident and injury which is in Class 9, surgeons' clothing which is in Class 10 or clothing for animals which is in Class 18.

Class 26

Lace and embroidery, ribbons and braid; buttons, hooks and eyes, pins and needles; artificial flowers.

Includes dressmakers' articles; badges for wear (other than precious metal badges).

Class 27

Carpets, rugs, mats and matting, linoleum and other materials for covering existing floors; wall hangings (non-textile).

Includes wallpaper.

Does not include mouse mats which are in Class 9, mats specifically shaped/adapted for vehicles which are in Class 12 or travellers' rugs which are in Class 24.

Class 28

Games and playthings; gymnastic and sporting articles not included in other classes; decorations for Christmas trees.

Includes hand-held computer games equipment which is self-contained (not adapted for use with TV receivers).

Does not include computer games equipment adapted for use with TV receivers or software for all types of electronic games which are in Class 9.

Class 29

Meat, fish, poultry and game; meat extracts; preserved, dried and cooked fruits and vegetables; jellies, jams, fruit sauces; eggs, milk and milk products; edible oils and fats.

Includes prepared meals and snacks whose main ingredients are proper to this class (e.g. soups and potato crisps).

Does not include sandwiches which are in Class 30 or foodstuffs for animals which are in Class 31.

Class 30

Coffee, tea, cocoa, sugar, rice, tapioca, sago, artificial coffee; flour and preparations made from cereals, bread, pastry and confectionery, ices; honey, treacle; yeast, baking-powder, salt, mustard; vinegar, sauces (condiments); spices; ice.

Includes prepared meals and snacks whose main ingredients are proper to this class (e.g. pizzas, pies and pasta dishes).

Does not include foodstuffs for animals which are in Class 31.

Class 31

Agricultural, horticultural and forestry products and grains not included in other classes; live animals; fresh fruits and vegetables, seeds, natural plants and flowers; foodstuffs for animals; malt.

Includes all food and beverages for animals.

Class 32

Beers; mineral and aerated waters and other non-alcoholic drinks; fruit drinks and fruit juices; syrups and other preparations for making beverages.

Includes shandy, de-alcoholised drinks, nonalcoholic beers and wines.

Does not include tea, coffee or chocolate-based beverages which are in Class 30.

Class 33

Alcoholic beverages (except beers).

Includes wines, spirits and liqueurs; alcopops.

Does not include beers which are in Class 32.

Class 34

Tobacco; smokers' articles; matches.

Includes lighters for smokers.

Services

Class 35

Advertising; business management; business administration; office functions.

Includes the organisation, operation and supervision of loyalty and incentive schemes; advertising services provided via the Internet; production of television and radio advertisements; accountancy; auctioneering; trade fairs; opinion polling; data processing; provision of business information; certain specific services provided by retailers.

Does not include raising finance for business which is in Class 36 or computer programming which is in Class 42.

Class 36

Insurance; financial affairs; monetary affairs; real estate affairs.

Includes building society services; banking (including home banking); stockbroking; financial services provided via the Internet; issuing of tokens of value in relation to bonus and loyalty schemes; provision of financial information.

Does not include accountancy which is in Class 35, lottery services which are in Class 41 or surveying and conveyancing services which are in Class 42.

Class 37

Building construction; repair; installation services.

Includes installation, maintenance and repair of computer hardware; painting and decorating.

Does not include installation, maintenance and repair of computer software which is in Class 42.

Class 38

Telecommunications.

Includes all telecommunications services (e.g. e-mail services and those provided for the Internet); providing user access to the Internet (service providers); operating of search engines.

Does not include creating, maintaining or hosting websites which are in Class 42.

Class 39

Transport; packaging and storage of goods; travel arrangement.

Includes distribution of electricity; travel information.

Does not include travel insurance which is in Class 36 or booking holiday accommodation which is in Class 43.

Class 40

Treatment of materials.

Includes the development, duplicating and printing of photographs; generation of electricity.

Class 41

Education; providing of training; entertainment; sporting and cultural activities.

Includes electronic games services provided by means of the Internet; the provision of online electronic publications and digital music (not downloadable) from the Internet.

Does not include downloadable online electronic publications or digital music which are in Class 9 or educational materials in printed form which are in Class 16.

Class 42

Scientific and technological services and research and design relating thereto; industrial analysis and research services; design and development of computer hardware and software.

Includes installation, maintenance and repair of computer software; computer consultancy services; design, drawing and commissioned writing for the compilation of websites; creating, maintaining and hosting the websites of others; compilation, creation and maintenance of a register of domain names; leasing of access time to a computer database on a dedicated line and not access provided by Internet Service Providers to databases in general which is in Class 38.

Does not include providing access to the Internet or portal services which are in Class 38.

Class 43

Services for providing food and drink; temporary accommodation.

Includes restaurant, bar and catering services; provision of holiday accommodation; booking and reservation services for restaurants and holiday accommodation.

Does not include provision of permanent accommodation which is in Class 36 or the arranging of travel by tourist agencies which is in Class 39.

Class 44

Medical services; veterinary services; hygienic and beauty care for human beings or animals; agriculture, horticulture and forestry services.

Includes dentistry services; medical analysis for diagnosis and treatment of people (such as x-ray examinations and taking of blood samples); pharmacy advice; garden design services.

Does not include ambulance transportation which is in Class 39, health clubs for physical exercise which are in Class 41, scientific research for medical purposes (such as research into cures for terminal diseases which is in Class 42), or retirement homes which are in Class 43.

Class 45

Security services for the protection of property and individuals; a limited range of personal services not covered in the other service classes.

Includes dating services; funeral and undertaking services; fire-fighting services; detective agency services; legal services.

Does not include educational services which are in Class 41 or beauty care services for human beings or animals which are in Class 44.

COPYRIGHT
No UK registration system

Unlike trade marks, under UK law copyright arises automatically when an original literary, dramatic, musical or artistic work is recorded in a permanent form, for example on paper, film or disk. There is no copyright registration system. Therefore, if an employee of yours creates a copyright work in the course of his employment, you as employer will own the copyright as soon as the work is created.

The international protection available for copyright works

Copyright is a territorial right, which means that you can only sue for infringement of UK copyright in the UK. Other countries have their own separate and distinct copyright laws.

It is likely that you will want to exploit your copyright work on a global basis, for example by using your artistic work (e.g. a logo) on your website or as part of your business in other countries. If you do want to use your UK copyright material internationally, what copyright protection will you receive in other countries? What recourse will you have if your work is reproduced in another country? Will you be able to prevent a third party in, for example, Brazil from copying your logo which was created in the UK?

Two international Conventions to which the UK is a signatory – the Berne Convention and the Universal Copyright Convention – provide answers to these questions. Both Conventions give a basic degree of protection for English copyright owners in other Convention countries. For example, the Conventions provide the same protection you would have received under Brazilian law had the copyright been created by a Brazilian national in Brazil, i.e. they provide you with the same rights as national authors.

The effect of these Conventions is that if you were to discover that, say, a Brazilian company has reproduced your UK copyright work in Brazil, you would have legal redress in Brazil because, as an English copyright owner, you would receive the equivalent Brazilian copyright protection.

In addition, the Conventions ensure that Convention countries provide nationals of other member countries with copyright protection without having to comply with local formalities which may be applicable in certain countries, such as registration, regardless of the fact that domestic nationals and/or works first published locally must comply with such local formalities.

Key countries which are signatories to the Conventions include Australia, Canada, China (excluding Hong Kong), France, Germany, Italy, Japan, Spain, the UK and the USA.

Use the © symbol

Although there are no formalities required to protect UK copyright, if you intend to exploit your copyright work internationally, you should include on your copyright work the © symbol together with the year of first publication and the name of the copyright owner. This is necessary to assist in securing the above copyright protection for the work in countries which are signatories to the Universal Copyright Convention without having to comply with local registration formalities in the Convention countries.

It is not necessary to include the © symbol to benefit from copyright protection in the UK or to bring UK infringement proceedings, but it is advisable to do so for the international reasons above.

The form of the notice should, for example, be 'Copyright © 2006 John Wiley & Sons Limited'.

DESIGNS

UK registration procedure

Applications to register a UK design are dealt with by the UK Patent Office.

In addition to providing general information about you, as applicant, and (where relevant) your legal representative, the application must include a note of the particular product(s) to which your design is intended to be applied or incorporated. The application must also be accompanied by a sample or representation of the design (either photos or drawings) which present an accurate and complete picture of your design.

In the case of decorative or non two-dimensional designs, your illustrations should show the design from a series of views, each labelled accordingly, e.g. 'perspective view from front, above and one side'. Descriptive footnotes are encouraged. Where registration of only part of a design is sought, an explanatory disclaimer must be included and the illustrations should clearly indicate the extent of the application for registration.

As applicant you are required to sign a declaration stating that you are the owner of the design and that you believe the design is 'new and has individual character'.

A small fixed application fee is payable to the Patent Office.

The Patent Office will give you a note of receipt and then examine the application within approximately two months. They will need to be satisfied that your design is not simply dictated by its technical function or does not contain any restricted emblems, such as the Royal Crown. Previously the Patent Office used to examine whether or not the design was new (i.e. had not already been made available to the public) and had individual character, but this is no longer the case because it was a very time consuming investigation which rarely resulted in objections being raised.

Once the Patent Office examination has been completed, your design application will either be accepted, in which case you will be sent a registration certificate, or you will receive an examination report from the Patent Office listing the objections.

There may be objections either because there was something wrong with the application itself or because the Patent Office believes the design does not qualify as a registered design. If you wish to contest this decision you must reply within two months or ask for an extension of time of up to a further three months.

Unlike with trade marks, third parties do not have the right to oppose the application itself. They do, however, have the right to apply for it to be 'invalidated' once it has been registered. The design is published in the *Patents and Designs Journal* and third parties often monitor this to see if there are any new designs they wish to have invalidated. The owner is of course informed of any invalidity action.

Third parties can apply for the registration to be invalidated on a number of grounds including on the basis that the design is not new (i.e. it has already been made available to the public), or that it lacks individual character because the overall impression the design gives is not different to the impression any previous design gives.

Your registration can be renewed every five years for a fixed fee which increases for each renewal.

Community registration procedure

Applications to register a community design are dealt with by the Office for Harmonisation in the Internal Market (OHIM) which is based in Alicante in Spain. Applications may be made in a number of languages including English.

As with design applications to the Patent Office, OHIM requires that a representation of your design (in either illustrative or photographic form) must accompany your community design application. There must be a minimum of one and a maximum of seven views of the graphical representation. In the case of applications for community design registration of a piece of material, at least five specimens must be provided in specific dimensions.

Your application can also describe the representation or specimen in up to 100 words. This description is purely illustrative and will not be published, nor does it affect the scope of protection of the community design, if successful.

An initial fixed fee is payable in euros together with additional (lower) fees if several applications are made together. There is also a separate publication fee which is payable up front. Application forms can be sent directly to OHIM or you can work through a national office such as the UK Patent Office.

Again there is an examination process with appeal rights if you are not immediately successful. The criteria by which the merits of the application will be assessed are substantially the same as those for an application to register a design with the UK Patent Office.

Additional reasons for refusal are that the subject matter:

- does not correspond with OHIM's definition of a design; or
- 'is contrary to public policy or to accepted principles or morality'. However, an application shall not be refused purely on the grounds of bad taste. This criterion therefore clearly contains an element of subjectivity.

The clearer the presentation of the design (through photos, plans etc.) the less likely it is that the examiner will need to query the design. You should also indicate the products that the design will be applied to.

A third party may contest your registration on the grounds that the design lacks novelty or individual character; that the holder is not the person or company entitled to the contested community design; that the design is in conflict with a prior design; that the design makes unauthorised use of a distinctive sign or work protected by copyright; or that the design makes improper use of, for example, the flag, badge or emblem belonging to a Member State.

Aside from the clear difference that a successful application for registration of a community design with OHIM will cover the entire EU, while registration of a design with the UK Patent Office will only cover the UK, OHIM also allows an applicant to request that the publication of the design be deferred for up to 30 months from the application date, whereas the UK Patent Office will only defer publication for 12 months. The benefit of this is that the applicant can keep 'blueprints' for a new design out of the public domain for a longer period of time and thus minimise any residual risk of unauthorised imitation prior to the launch of the product and even afterwards.

Chapter

3

·····································

HOUSEKEEPING YOUR TRADE MARK PORTFOLIO

Housekeeping ain't no joke.

Louisa May Alcott, *Little Women*

HOUSEKEEPING TIPS FOR PRESERVING AND PROTECTING YOUR TRADE MARK PORTFOLIO

Register your trade marks in the name of the same proprietor

Take a consistent approach to the identity of the proprietor when registering your trade marks.

Where there is a group company structure, you should ideally, subject to the goodwill consideration below, make all your applications in the name of the parent or holding company. This should help ensure, for example, that trade marks do not end up in the name of a company that has been transferred out of your group or dissolved.

It is important that the proprietor of the trade mark is also the owner of the goodwill and reputation in the mark in question. With the exception of exclusive licensees, it is only the registered proprietor who can commence trade mark infringement proceedings. It is therefore essential to register the correct corporate entity as the proprietor. You do not want a separate corporate entity to own the goodwill in the same mark because then one company will have to bring trade mark infringement proceedings and another company passing off proceedings, although this can be cured with the appropriate transfer of rights intra-company.

In all cases, it should be you as brand owner who is the registered proprietor of the trade mark and not your distributor or licensee. If trade marks have been registered in the name of licensees or distributors rather than the brand owner, you ought to consider the need to transfer those registrations into the name of the brand owner.

Be consistent when using your trade marks

To achieve a consistent and unified brand position and to protect your trade mark registrations against revocation for non-use, it is crucial that every use of your trade mark utilises the exact typeface, graphic and configuration as that which you have registered. For example, you should ensure that you are using exactly the same company logo across all your operations, from your letterheads and invoices to your actual products. Use of even a slight variant could potentially open you up to attack by unscrupulous competitors claiming that the boundaries are vague and up for grabs.

If you have a significant trade mark portfolio you should put together logo and trade mark usage reference guides for your licensees and distributors as well as your commercial and marketing people. The following is a checklist of points that should be considered when drawing up such guidelines:

- How big should the trade mark or logo be on the product in question? You should give a minimum size and then ensure that all enlargements are in proportion.
- Show, by way of example, the minimum clear space that must be kept around the logo or mark.
- Give the correct angle and centre point that the logo or mark should be placed in.
- Is there a particular font/typeface that should be used?
- What colours can be used (both for the actual mark and the background)? Be specific and include, for example, any colour schemes that can or cannot be used.
- Is there a particular position where the logo or mark should appear on certain materials (for example, on stationery, advertisement or brochures)?
- Should the mark always come first when combined with other words?
- You should state that the entirety of the logo or mark should be visible. For example, use of just the first letter (even if this is stylised) should not be permitted (unless this is also registered as a trade mark).

- If applicable, state which particular trade marks and logos should be used and when.
- Set out clear examples of what must not be done to the mark.

Whether or not you decide to produce such a guide, the following actions should ensure that your trade marks remain distinctive and reduce the chance of attack by third parties:

- Your trade mark should never be pluralised, abbreviated, shortened, hyphenated or misspelt, unless those versions of the mark are also registered as trade marks.
- Your trade mark should never be altered, modified, split or distorted nor used in a way that affects the mark's legibility or distinctive appearance. If you use a mark in a different form to that in which it is registered, then your registration will be susceptible to revocation and may not protect the use you are actually making against infringement.
- Wherever possible, and especially when it incorporates a logo, graphic or other design, your trade mark should never vary in either design or colour.
- As explained on page 10, you should always emphasise a word or logo's trade mark status and follow it with a trade mark notice (® or ™ as appropriate) and a note that the particular mark is a trade mark owned and/or registered

by you. This applies to all products, packaging, advertising and promotional material, web pages and documentation.

- When using a trade mark in literary materials (brochures, company reports, marketing materials), distinguish it from the rest of the text by using a different typeface (preferably the typeface as registered), capitalising it or putting the mark in quotation marks.
- The above rules apply not only to your products, advertising, labelling and external documentation but also to your internal correspondence.

Do not allow your trade marks to become generic

If you allow your trade mark to become the generic or common everyday name for your product or service, you risk having your trade mark revoked or invalidated on the ground that it is no longer capable of distinguishing your goods or services from those of other third parties. You may also struggle to show that you have a sufficient reputation in the mark to support a passing off action. This could leave you with no rights in your mark while, correspondingly, allowing your competitors to use the mark with impunity.

To avoid your trade mark becoming generic, you should use it only as an adjective, never as a noun or verb as this will lead to it being referred to in common parlance as a generic term (examples of once distinctive trade marks which have now become unprotectable generic nouns include 'Linoleum' and 'Escalator'). For example:

- correct: 'The Hoover vacuum cleaner is well made'
- incorrect: 'The Hoover is well made'

- correct: 'Do you need to vacuum your house with a Hoover vacuum cleaner?'
- incorrect: 'Do you need to hoover your house?'

You should also not allow third parties to use your trade mark as the common name for a particular product. Any misuse of your mark in advertising or marketing media by third parties should be addressed immediately.

Conduct regular trade mark audits

If a registered trade mark has not been used for a continuous period of five years or more, it will become vulnerable to revocation for non-use. In such circumstances, a third party wanting to register or use the same or a similar mark may be able to have your mark removed from the register.

It is therefore important that you conduct regular (ideally annual) audits of your trade mark portfolio to determine which, if any, trade marks are not being used any more, and if so, whether or not the five-year period is close to expiry. Ideally, you should also keep records of the use being made of each trade mark (e.g. where has it been used, when, how, what was the marketing expenditure involved?).

If you no longer use a particular registered trade mark and you do not envisage doing so in the future, you should consider allowing the registration to lapse rather than incurring renewal fees.

In addition to guarding against revocation for non-use, your audits should also consider the following questions:

- Are there any trade marks (or indeed registered designs or domain names) that are coming up for renewal? If so, do you want to renew them or let them lapse?
- Are all relevant trade mark classes covered? As explained on page 52, there are 45 classes of goods and services available. You should periodically consider whether or not your existing registrations are adequate and whether any further classes need to be covered. Your business may have moved on since the date of registration.

- Are your trade marks being used consistently and only in the form in which they are registered?
- Do you have adequate registrations for all relevant markets? With the exception of community trade marks and Madrid Protocol registrations, registration systems are territorial. You need to consider whether or not you have adequate registrations in place for each and every territory within which your goods or services are sold, not just your main territories or those territories where you know there are infringement problems. You never know where the next infringement will be.

Certificates

When the trade mark registration process is complete, you will receive a trade mark certificate from the relevant Registry detailing the date of registration, the representation of the mark, the classes in which it has been registered, and the name and address of the proprietor. You should keep all of your original trade mark certificates in a safe and secure place.

Keep accurate and accessible records

As a brand owner, you do not want to be unnecessarily delayed in pursuing infringers due to difficulties encountered in accessing accurate records of your various trade mark registrations held by subsidiaries in different territories. You should put in place a system (e.g. on your intranet) whereby any group company can access, in a consistent format, summary information of all registrations. It is therefore important to keep an accurate and up to date record of the key details of each of your trade marks registrations in one easily accessible place which lists the following information for each registered trade mark:

- if it is a device mark, a visual representation of the trade mark as registered; if it is a word mark, say so
- country of registration: is it a national registration or a CTM/Madrid Protocol registration?
- registration number (if it is only at the application stage, then the application number)
- classification of goods/services covered by the registration
- priority date (this is usually the date the application was made)
- next renewal date (this is very important and should be highlighted in bold)
- name of registered proprietor
- details of any registered licensees
- details of the trade mark agent responsible for the registration (name of firm and contact name of individual dealing, address, telephone number and e-mail address)

- details of your employee responsible for the registration and renewal (see page 99 re chain of command)

Renewal dates

Provided it has been used regularly and has not lost its distinctiveness (e.g. by becoming generic), a trade mark is automatically renewable for successive 10-year periods. It is vital that you keep track of your trade mark registrations' expiry dates and that you arrange for your marks, if you are still using them, to be renewed in good time before they expire. Failure to pay a renewal fee on time could result in your trade mark being struck off the Trade Marks Register.

External counsel and trade mark agents send their clients standard form and automatic renewal reminders, although it is a good idea also to keep your own central record of all renewal dates. Don't forget to keep a note of the renewal dates of your other registrable intellectual property rights, such as domain names and registered designs.

Chapter

4

. . . .

IP AND YOUR EMPLOYEES

Did he smile his work to see?

William Blake, *The Tyger*

IP AND EMPLOYEES
What to include in your employment contracts and why

Most of your employees will, during the course of their employment, create work containing intellectual property rights. Some of this will not be of particular value to the business (for example, the copyright in your staff's day-to-day correspondence). However, employees do regularly create valuable intellectual property for their employers. This will obviously be the case where this is their job, as with marketing, creative and R&D staff, who devise new products, technologies, designs, marketing initiatives and advertising campaigns. But it is also true even in industries not traditionally seen to be IP focused. For example, in all companies staff will produce presentations and marketing materials and create databases. Such work will attract copyright and possibly database right and design right protection.

In creative industries in particular, staff will often be creating highly valuable assets. For example, writers employed by a television production company will write scripts, computer programmers who work for an IT company will write source code for new software and creative personnel who work for a media company will produce marketing and advertising materials. All of these will be valuable assets protected by intellectual property rights.

Fortunately, IP rights generally belong automatically to the employer, as long as the work has been created in the course of the employee's employment. However, it is always a good idea to ensure that there is a clause in your employment contracts assigning to you as employer all of the intellectual property rights in work created by your employees in the course of their employment.

Not all of your staff may be aware of who is an employee and who is a freelance agent. There is therefore a danger that a freelance agent (and not an employee) may be creating intellectual property rights in a valuable asset that your business may need in the future and so you should always ensure that all contracts with your contractors assign to you the intellectual property rights created in their work.

Confidentiality clauses

As a matter of course, your employment contracts should also contain a confidentiality clause prohibiting your employees from sharing any confidential information relating to your business (e.g. new inventions, designs, concepts) with anyone else.

Although a duty of confidence will be implied by law into employment contracts and may also be implied in other non-employment circumstances, it is not advisable to rely on this to protect your information as it may not have the necessary 'quality of confidence' required by law or perhaps the circumstances in which it was disclosed may not have imposed an obligation to keep it secret. Without including a specific clause in your employee contracts setting out your employees' obligations and defining what you regard as 'confidential information', the only information that will definitely be protected is information that is so secret that it can reasonably be described as a trade secret. The test is a high one and accordingly you should always ensure that your employment contracts and your terms of engagement with freelance workers contain express confidentiality obligations.

If there is confidential information which is of particular importance to your business (typically, newly invented technology), you should consider restricting access to it to certain key members of staff only.

Moral rights and waiver

As explained on page 19, moral rights include the right of an author of a copyright work to object to

distortions of that work and the right to be identified as the author of the work. Moral rights waivers
are far more important when you use freelances
because employees are not entitled to moral rights
in respect of work done in the course of their
employment contract. However, for reasons of
caution and prudence, you will often see employment contracts containing a clause confirming
that the employee expressly waives his moral
rights.

Commissioned work/Contractors

As explained on page 16, extra care needs to be
taken when commissioning non-employees to do
creative work for you. This is because if someone
is not your employee then, by law, they will own,
in particular, copyright in the works you commission them to do.

You will therefore need to ensure that there is an
assignment of the freelance's IP rights in the
terms of engagement. This does not need to be a
separate document; one paragraph in the terms
assigning all rights (present and future) in the
work created for you will suffice.

If the freelance creator will not agree to assign to
you the intellectual property in the work, then
you should ensure that you have an irrevocable,

royalty-free and perpetual licence to use the work. This means that you will have unrestricted access to use the work without further payment.

If the contractor is prepared to assign his IP rights to you, or even if he is only prepared to license them, his contract should also contain a waiver of his moral rights.

Your contract with a contractor who is creating original works for you should also contain a warranty that the work he submits does not infringe anyone else's IP rights and, in the event that it does, an indemnity in your favour in respect of any litigation that ensues.

Communicating to all employees the importance of IP

It is vital that all of your employees, from your receptionists to your executives, are aware of the importance of IP to your business so that, for example, when they spot counterfeit goods during their time off, or when they take calls from consumers who have been confused by an advertisement for your competitor's goods, they know what to do.

Ideally you should have a written IP policy to guarantee a consistent approach across the business and so that all employees understand:

- what rights you own and don't own
- which are your core brands
- what your brand strategy is
- what activity will not be tolerated, e.g. competitors using your trade marks/advertising style/packaging
- who is responsible for which IP (see below re chain of command)
- who your external advisers are (e.g. solicitors and trade mark/patent agents)
- what your licensing/franchising strategy is (see pages 102–112)
- how your IP work is coordinated with your other domestic/foreign offices
- what to do if they learn of any infringements of your rights
- the need for speed in pursuing infringements (see page 151)

Chain of command

You should ensure that there is a visible chain of command so that everyone in your company knows who has responsibility for:

- particular brands or products
- particular territories
- trade mark applications and renewals (both domestic and foreign)
- registered design and/or patent applications (both domestic and foreign)

- licensing/franchising issues and the appointment of freelances
- monitoring competitor activity (e.g. advertising, websites, brochures, launches) to ensure that they do not infringe your rights
- enforcement work when staff learn about infringements of your rights
- handling claims against the company for infringements of other people's IP
- deciding whether or not to sue/defend
- instructing external counsel
- IP issues in acquisitions or general commercial contracts

Chapter

5

....

EXPLOITATION OF YOUR IP

The attempt to keep out evil doctrine by licensing is like the exploit of that gallant man who thought to keep out the cows by shutting the park gates.

John Milton, *Areopagitica*

EXPLOITATION OF YOUR IP

What is the difference between a licence and an assignment?

If you do not wish to undertake the exploitation of your brand yourself, then the options which give you a financial return are either (1) to sell the asset for a capital sum (by way of assignment) or (2) to ask someone else to exploit it for you (under a licensing arrangement).

A sale (i.e. an outright assignment of your rights) should be relatively straightforward. Provided you can demonstrate that you own all of the relevant rights, then as between a willing buyer and a willing seller the question is largely one of price. You may additionally be asked to enter into a number of warranties to substantiate your ownership. A sale obviously has a significant benefit to your company's immediate cash position.

An assignment of a registered trade mark must be in writing and signed by or legitimately held on behalf of the owner. A verbal agreement to assign may be enough to transfer what are known as the 'equitable rights' in the registered trade mark – that is, the right to benefit from the mark and have it transferred to you in due course – but it does leave the outstanding headache of the actual transfer and is best avoided. In practical terms, the same is true of unregistered trade marks, designs and copyright works.

There is, however, an alternative to a sale, which is to retain your ownership, and at the same time license a third party to undertake the exploitation of the brand on your behalf. Subject to certain constraints of EU law on free movement of goods and services, licences can be created in any number of product categories and territories. In this way, you as licensor have the opportunity to hold onto an asset which you hope will grow in value long term, largely through the efforts of your licensees, as well as to see the brand develop in territories where you may not have the expertise, inclination or resource to develop it yourself. From the licensee's perspective, it can tap into what may be a wider global brand that it could not otherwise afford to purchase outright. You as licensor derive a licence fee by way of royalty, based generally on a percentage of sales, but each deal can set whatever payment mechanism it wishes, as there are no hard and fast rules.

Like assignments, licences of registered trade marks must be in writing, but verbal licences of the equitable rights may be sufficient to start the licensing process. However, such verbal licences cause uncertainty and difficulty as time passes and the original terms are forgotten. If the terms are down on paper, then they stand a far better chance of being remembered and enforced.

Exclusive/Non-exclusive

It is important for both a licensor and licensee to be clear as to whether or not the IP licence granted is exclusive or non-exclusive in relation to each particular product category, territory, time period or whatever other field of operation that is to be granted.

If a licence is granted on an exclusive basis, then for that territory and term, no person other than the licensee may exploit the brand. This includes the licensor, so if you do in fact intend to operate the brand yourself but wish to nominate only one other licensee to work alongside you, then exclusivity is *not* for you. It follows that a non-exclusive licence is capable of being exploited by more than one licensee as well as the licensor if necessary.

There is often confusion between *exclusive* and *sole* licensees. The difference is that if a licence is granted on a sole basis then the licensor as well as that one licensee is able to exploit the brand. Some licences attempt to grant rights on a sole and exclusive basis – while this may have meaning in other jurisdictions, under English law it doesn't make sense.

Exclusiv e licensees of registered trade marks are afforded extra protection in that they are entitled to:

- enforce their licence automatically against future owners of the registered trade marks
- call on the owner to commence proceedings against infringers, failing which the licensee may bring proceedings in its own name
- a share in any monetary damages where the court thinks the licensee has suffered as a result of any infringement

Registration implications

A licensee or assignee should generally always register a licence or an assignment. In the case of registered trade marks, until an application has been made for registration of a licence, a licensee can take no action against:

- a third party who acquires another licence in ignorance of a prior licence, even if the aggrieved first licensee thinks its rights are exclusive

- a third party who acquires ownership of the underlying trade mark

There is one other significant benefit to registering a licence or assignment of a registered trade mark as regards infringement claims against third parties. If the registration is not undertaken within six months of the licence or assignment, the licensee/assignee can only claim damages for infringement from the date of registration of its interest.

In the case of patents, again a licence which is not registered will not have effect against a person who subsequently purchases the patent and seeks to deny the existence of the licence on the basis that he had purchased it believing it not to have been licensed.

For all other intellectual property rights which do not form part of a registered system, such as copyright, design rights, unregistered trade marks and goodwill, the licensee/assignee can take action against infringers from the date of transfer (subject, in the case of a licence, to the terms of that licence).

Registrations by rogue licensees

If you are the owner of a trade mark in the UK, and one of your licensees tries to hijack your mark by registering it in its own name without your permission, then, provided that you take action within three years of becoming aware of the registration, you can object to that registration so as either to declare it invalid or require that it be registered in your name instead.

Standard protective licensing provisions

A licensed intellectual property right remains an asset on your balance sheet, therefore you must take appropriate steps to protect that asset, otherwise it will lose its financial value. If the rights are licensed, then it is important to ensure that any licence agreement places the onus, as far as possible, upon the licensee to look after your rights for you. This will include a number of common provisions:

• *Be clear as to the scope of the licence*: can the licensee subcontract, sublicense, appoint an agent or distributor, in each case with or without your approval? Do you want to know who such third parties are? What type of ethical policies do they practise, especially off-shore-based manufacturers? What happens to overruns from their factories – do they go straight 'out the back door'? Don't accept that it's none of your business provided the goods arrive on time and to specification: you as brand owner have the right to be involved. Make sure you have extensive audit rights to check what your licensee is doing.

- *Rights of approval*: the product or service that bears your brand must meet quality criteria for you to be able to say that genuinely you control the brand. These criteria must be set out in the licence agreement. Do you want to see products as samples or completed items? Do you have a right to audit designs, factories, retail outlets? Do not simply count the royalty cheques – know the details! It is your brand and you are responsible for it. Ensure that you, and not your licensees, retain control over your trade marks and how they are used by way of a usage reference guide (see page 83).

- *Identification of infringing activities*: the licensee, as operator in the relevant marketplace, will normally be best placed to identify where competitors or other parties are using the licensor's IP rights to try to gain a competitive advantage, a free benefit or both. To this extent your licensee becomes your eyes and ears. As soon as a licensee identifies or becomes aware of any form of infringement of your rights then it should be under an express obligation to report it to you, giving you sufficient details in order that you can assess the situation (preferably in a pre-agreed reporting format) and decide how best to proceed.

- *The decision as to how to enforce*: even though the usual position would be to protect your rights at any cost, there may be situations where, by dint of circumstance or for practical reasons, there is no genuine or proportionate benefit in you expending the money to enforce rights against a third party infringer. It may be that you decide not to enforce at all, or perhaps that you only wish to require that third party to desist from infringing rather than actually taking court proceedings against them for damages. As brand owner, this decision should be yours alone to make, and therefore express provision should be made in your contract with the licensee. This is particularly so where exclusive licences are granted as the exclusive licensee might otherwise seek to rely on its statutory rights to take such action itself.

The licence agreement should reinforce the fact that the licensee gains no rights in your brand other than those acquired under the licence. Be clear that:

- all rights (e.g. goodwill) arising from the use of the brand in the course of the licensee's business should pass to you as brand owner
- you alone have the right to extend any registration in any different territory or as a result of any extension of the brand itself

- the licensee endorses on his products and packaging the fact that the brand is in fact licensed to him from you
- the licensee will apply any labelling or identification tags, security swing tickets etc. to his products if requested
- the licensee will give you all due assistance in maintaining your brand portfolio as and when required

Such rights, along with any other bespoke requirements which are deemed necessary in the circumstances, should be included alongside general warranties from the licensee:

- as to the manner in which it will undertake the exploitation of your brand, for instance ensuring that everything is done in accordance with local laws and regulations
- to meet sales/roll-out targets
- to adhere to any brand guidelines which are issued and generally not to do anything which may prejudice or have a detrimental effect on the brand or your reputation as licensor

Franchising

As an extension to the general concept of licensing, some brand owners offer the opportunity for franchising. This is often seen in the retail sector where the rights to open a shop selling a particular brand of clothing in a particular environment is granted, or in the food industry where there is a set format for restaurant layout and menu.

In such cases, the licence should contain not only the right to use the brand but also the obligation to act in accordance with a certain model for operating the business. This is generally encapsulated within a franchise manual which is an extremely detailed document covering all aspects of the business and ensuring that that business not only starts off on the right foot, but continues to operate according to a set programme and is in a suitable state for transfer or termination at the end of the term. Franchising is generally undertaken on a personal basis, identifying the individual person who has the energy, drive and brand-fit qualities.

Mortgaging/Selling off unused IP

Maintaining an IP portfolio necessarily involves time and commitment, both from management and from external advisors (e.g. solicitors and trade mark agents). As such, there is little point in 'squatting' on unused IP when this can be sold off by way of an assignment to create added capital value. It is therefore advisable to conduct regular audits of your IP rights to consider which rights you no longer use or want. If you can find a willing purchaser who sees an opportunity to exploit the brand in a way in which you either do not wish to or somehow cannot do, and that exploitation will not impinge on your future business model, then it can be easy money.

An alternative is to mortgage the IP (also known as 'syndication'). This is most often seen in the music industry, where the rights to future royalties from copyrighted songs are mortgaged to a bank or other institution. The bank pays out a capital sum now, against the right to recoup that sum through future royalty income from those rights which continue to be exploited either by the brand owner or by a third party. Necessarily, the capital sum paid out now is lower than the actual value of the royalties over time, but the benefit of receiving that capital sum now can in some instances be extremely welcome for use in other projects.

Chapter

6

· ·

POLICING
YOUR IP

I am as vigilant as a cat to steal cream.
William Shakespeare, *Henry IV Part 1*

POLICING YOUR IP

Why is it important to monitor your IP for potential third party infringements?

If you discover that a third party is trying to piggy-back on your hard-won reputation, or that counterfeiters are eating into your bottom line, you will want to take swift and effective enforcement action against them.

It is therefore of critical importance that when a third party applies to register or starts using a trade mark, domain name, patent or design which conflicts with yours, or is dealing in works which infringe your copyright, you become aware of such applications or use as swiftly as possible, because any such registration or use could result in brand confusion, loss of revenue or even loss of a particular market. Advance notice of potentially infringing activity will put you in the best possible position to oppose any application for registration or to prevent the infringement, for example by way of an injunction (see page 162).

How can you find out if somebody is infringing your intellectual property rights?

There are a number of policing solutions you can employ in order to detect, track and prevent infringers and their infringing activities. Broadly, these can be categorised under the following three headings:

- utilising governmental/public agencies and prosecuting authorities
- engaging private service providers
- employing 'self-help'

Which governmental or public agencies can help you?

HM Revenue and Customs (R&C)

In the UK, there is a statutory system under which you, as owner of intellectual property rights, in particular trade marks and copyright works, may file notices with R&C asking them to seize infringing goods being imported into the country.

R&C operates two systems: one governing goods arriving into the UK from within the European Economic Area (EEA), and one for goods arriving into the UK from the rest of the world.

Goods arriving from outside the EEA: in this case, R&C will only be able to assist in relation to goods which infringe either your trade marks or your copyright. The notification procedure is as follows:

- R&C require you to complete a form detailing your name, the name and address of the owner of the copyright/trade mark and as much information as possible about the consignment under suspicion, such as the expected arrival date and its expected place of importation.
- There is a small fee payable for this service, and R&C reserve the right to request other security and indemnities from you.
- This is a service which should only be used where you have a reason to suspect that specific copyright or trade mark infringing goods are being imported, and is not a means of generally monitoring shipments for potentially infringing goods; it is not a watching service. However, if R&C does obtain infringing goods it has considerable powers to assist you in preventing the infringing goods from making it onto the market.
- Where goods fitting the notified description are intercepted by R&C, R&C may detain them. R&C must then inform the importer and the brand owner that the goods have been intercepted and will send a sample to the rights owner for inspection.

Goods arriving from within the EEA: you are entitled to lodge an application with R&C to prohibit delivery of counterfeit and pirated goods which infringe your trade marks, copyright or patents, so long as you hold a community trade mark, a registered community design or a European patent in the relevant product. The procedure is as follows:

- You must complete a Form C1340 which is an application for R&C to monitor goods arriving into the UK, or alternatively Form C1340A which is an application for customs authorities in two or more EEA member states (as specified by you) to monitor goods arriving at their respective ports of entry. You must provide your details, details about the owner of the intellectual property right, and as much specific information as possible to assist in the identification of the offending goods.
- R&C requests at least 30 days' notice (where possible) but there is no up-front fee. Note, however, that they reserve the right to charge any storage or destruction costs they incur. Applications are valid for 12 months and if a seizure of counterfeit or pirated goods does occur, R&C has powers to detain and, if appropriate, destroy the infringing goods.
- If R&C is satisfied that the goods do infringe your intellectual property, R&C will seize the goods and give warning to the importer, who is then entitled to contest the action.
- Where goods are found to be infringing they will be destroyed or disposed of.

Trading Standards

Local authorities have a statutory duty, through their Trading Standards Officers, to enforce the Trade Descriptions Act 1968 and the anti-counterfeiting provisions in the Trade Marks Act 1994 and the Copyright Designs & Patents Act 1988. Trading Standards Officers can therefore bring criminal proceedings against infringers.

Trading Standards, although government-run, is structured on a localised basis. In order to find the contact details for your relevant Trading Standards Officer, visit www.tradingstandards.gov.uk and enter your postcode. For practical reasons you may usually wish to contact the Trading Standards Officer in the area where your business is located, but you can also request assistance from the Trading Standards Officer nearest to the infringing party's premises if you prefer.

Trading Standards Officers have powers to make test purchases and to enter premises to inspect and seize goods and documents. Where there are reasonable grounds to believe an offence has been or is about to be committed, Trading Standards Officers, if refused entry to premises, can obtain warrants to search such premises.

If therefore you do not want to incur the cost and management time of pursuing civil litigation, a more cost effective option might be to report an infringer of your copyright, trade mark, design or patent to Trading Standards. The advantage is that the cost of the prosecution is borne by the state rather than by you the brand owner. But the disadvantages are that: you lose control of the action; there is no guarantee that Trading Standards will elect to prosecute as they have to justify spending taxpayers' money; and you will not receive any compensation from criminal proceedings although the infringer may be subject to a penalty or imprisonment.

The police

Counterfeiting and piracy are arrestable offences, which means that the police often join forces with Trading Standards Officers and R&C to investigate and prosecute criminal IP infringements.

How can private service providers help you monitor your intellectual property for infringements?

Watching services

The most common use of external, private service providers by brand owners seeking to monitor their intellectual property for third party infringements is to employ a watching service.

'Watching' is the term used to describe the process of regular searching of intellectual property registers for applications made by third parties to register trade marks, patents, designs or domain names which may be similar or identical to yours, or which may convey a similar impression or idea, and which you would not like your competitors to register or use.

The reason why this can be so valuable is that, although in the UK applicants for registered trade marks, designs and patents must satisfy the relevant registry that there is no prior identical or substantially similar registration in existence, the same cannot be said of certain other jurisdictions, which do not conduct a thorough search of the relevant register and may allow any mark to be registered despite the existence of prior identical or substantially similar registrations. Equally, while it is technically impossible for a third party to obtain a domain name identical to yours, a domain name almost identical to yours may be obtained and used to take advantage of the reputation built up in your website and cause confusion in the minds of your potential customers.

In other words, registration is not in every jurisdiction a guarantee of protection against applications for conflicting rights and steps must therefore be taken to prevent the registration of conflicting intellectual property.

Watching services can be implemented worldwide or in particular countries of interest to you, in a particular field of interest and in relation to a named competitor. Watching services are now sophisticated enough to pick up trade mark applications for shapes, smells, sounds, slogans, gestures and colours.

Watching services are offered by a wide range of professionals who deal with intellectual property matters. Law firms and firms of patent attorneys and trade mark agents will have standard rates for performing the searches. Costs will vary according to the scope, jurisdiction and regularity of searches, but given the importance of such searches they are relatively inexpensive.

Industry bodies and other anti-counterfeiting bodies

There are a number of other bodies that offer information and practical assistance in relation to counterfeiting and piracy. A selection is as follows:

• Alliance Against Counterfeiting & Piracy (AACP) – www.allianceagainstiptheft.co.uk

- Anti Copying in Design (ACID) – www.acid. uk.com
- Anti-Counterfeiting Group (ACG) – www. a-cg.com
- British Music Rights – www.bmr.org
- British Phonographic Industry (BPI) – www.bpi. co.uk
- British Video Association – www.bva.org.uk
- Business Software Alliance (BSA) – www.bsa. org
- The Entertainment and Leisure Software Publishers Association (ELSPA) – www.elspa.com
- Federation Against Copyright Theft (FACT) – www.fact-uk.org.uk
- Federation Against Software Theft (FAST) – www.fast.org.uk
- International Chamber of Commerce (ICC) Counterfeiting Intelligence Bureau (CIB) – www.iccwbo.org/ccs/menu_cib_bureau.asp
- International Federation of Phonographic Industries (IFPI) – www.ifpi.org

Private investigators

In some cases, you may want to retain a private investigator to:

- use pretext calls to try to find out the true identity and contact details of the trader in question

- make trap purchases via a front company so that you do not risk revealing yourself
- trace the chain of supply of the infringing goods
- investigate a factory that you believe to be manufacturing infringing goods

Self-help

In addition to having in place R&C notifications, good relations with your local Trading Standards Officers and a watching service, there are of course certain steps that you yourself can take to monitor parties who you suspect are or may in the future be infringing your intellectual property rights. Such steps include the following:

- *Test purchases*: if you learn about potential infringing activity, for example that a market stall is selling counterfeit goods or that a website is offering goods bearing your trade mark which you suspect may not have been licensed, then an obvious first step before you call your lawyers is to make a test purchase in order to identify whether the goods actually are infringing goods. In case the matter goes to litigation, it is important that you retain all evidence of such test purchases, including not only the goods themselves but also the receipts. If you visit a store to make your test purchase, you should also prepare a contemporaneous note of your visit:

when did you go; to which store address; what did you see; roughly how many infringing goods were on offer; at what price; how prominently were they displayed?

- *Website monitoring*: as part of your brand strategy, somebody within your company should have responsibility for conducting regular (ideally weekly) internet searches against your key brand names. Not only will this disclose whether or not competitors are using your trade marks as metatags for their own websites, but it is also a good way of monitoring any use made by third parties of your trade marks in the content of their websites generally (e.g. they may be selling counterfeit or unlicensed goods which infringe your trade marks or copyright). If there are particular third parties with whom you have had infringement difficulties previously, their own websites should of course also be monitored on a regular basis. If you find a website on which counterfeit or unlicensed products are being sold, print off the relevant pages of the website or, even better, save the offending website to your hard drive or CD-ROM so that you can access it at a later date if the website's content is changed or if the site has been deactivated. This will be important evidence of infringement in due course.

- *eBay monitoring*: major brand owners should also monitor auction websites such as eBay.

eBay is cautious to make it clear to participants that it does not verify that sellers have a right to sell the item. Instead, eBay operates a Verify Rights Owner programme that allows brand owners the opportunity to identify and request the removal of infringing items.

- *Use your employees as IP guardians*: if your employees are aware of the IP that you own and how it is infringed, they, as consumers, can be invaluable in recognising and reporting infringements of your rights. You should consider motivating your employees with incentives for discovering infringements.
- *Public awareness initiatives*: a good way to deter future infringers is to get your PR vehicle into action and publicise previous successes against infringers. You can also encourage customers to become your eyes and ears by providing, on your goods, a contact number to which to report possible infringements.

Chapter

7

. . . .

HOW ARE YOUR IP RIGHTS INFRINGED?

The ordinary people must lead a life of strict obedience and have no right to transgress the law because . . . they are ordinary.
Fyodor Dostoevsky, *Crime and Punishment*

REGISTERED TRADE MARKS

Advantages of registering

The benefits of incurring the costs of registering your trade marks become apparent as and when you need to enforce them. For a trade mark infringement action, unlike with a passing off claim, it is not always necessary to prove:

- that you have reputation and goodwill in your mark
- that consumers are confused into believing that there is a connection between your mark and the competing mark

Acts of civil infringement

In order to establish that a third party has infringed your trade mark, you first have to establish that the third party has used its potentially infringing mark in the course of trade. This includes:

- affixing the mark to goods or packaging
- selling or offering for sale goods under the mark
- stocking such goods for the purpose of selling or offering them for sale
- importing or exporting goods under the mark
- using the mark on business papers or in advertising

The question of precisely how a trade mark must be 'used' by a third party in order to infringe has vexed both English and European Union judges. Does the infringing use have to be use 'as a trade mark', use as a 'badge of origin', or some more general use? This question requires specific advice on a case by case basis.

Infringement of your registered trade mark will occur where, in the course of trade, a third party does any of the following:

- uses a mark *identical* to your registered trade mark in relation to goods or services *identical* to those covered by your registration
- uses a mark *identical* to your registered trade mark in relation to goods or services *similar* to those covered by your registration (where the public is likely to be confused)
- uses a mark *similar* to your registered trade mark in relation to goods or services *identical* to those covered by your registration (where the public is likely to be confused)
- uses a mark *similar* to your registered trade mark in relation to goods or services *similar* to those covered by your registration (where the public is likely to be confused)
- uses a mark *identical or similar* to your 'well-known' registered trade mark in relation to goods or services *identical, similar or dissimilar* to those covered by your registration (where

the use takes unfair advantage of, or is detrimental to, the distinctive character or repute of
your 'well-known' mark). You will be able to
establish unfair advantage or detriment if you
can show that the third party's mark will in
some way blur, tarnish or dilute the distinctive
character of your mark

Your registered trade mark will *not* be infringed
where the third party is, in good faith:

• using his own registered trade mark in relation
  to the goods or services for which it has been
  registered: this deals with the position where
  there are concurrent registrations of similar
  marks, although in that situation you may be
  able to challenge the registration of the competing mark
• using his own name or address: known as the
  'own name defence'
• using your trade mark to do nothing more than
  describe your goods or services or their attributes
  (e.g. their quality, intended purpose, geographi-
  cal origin)
• using your trade mark to describe his accessories or spare parts for your goods
• using your trade mark in a comparative advertisement, so long as the comparison is honest
  and not significantly misleading

Criminal trade mark offences

As an alternative to civil proceedings, you might want to consider reporting an infringer to Trading Standards which may in turn decide to prosecute the infringer criminally and which also have powers to execute search warrants. Although this may be a more cost effective means of dealing with infringers because the cost of the prosecution is borne by the state rather than by you as brand owner, the disadvantages are that: you lose control of the enforcement of your trade marks; there is no guarantee that Trading Standards will elect to prosecute; you will not receive any compensation from criminal proceedings although the infringer may be subject to a penalty or imprisonment.

The criminal offences of trade mark infringement are targeted at those who seek to make and/or sell counterfeit goods. Broadly, they can be broken down into two categories:

- possessing or dealing with infringing goods, with a view to personal gain or with intent to cause loss to the trade mark proprietor
- making, possessing or dealing with an article designed for making infringing goods, with a view to personal gain or with intent to cause loss to the trade mark proprietor

It is a defence to criminal trade mark infringement for the alleged infringer to establish that he
believed, on reasonable grounds, that his use was
not an infringement of your registered trade
mark.

A person found guilty of criminal trade mark infringement can be fined or sentenced to a maximum of 10 years in prison.

The grey market goods problem

The parallel importing of grey market goods poses
a major problem for brand owners. When third
party importers purchase your genuine, trade
marked goods in one country where you intended
them to be sold, but then import them into another
country where you did not want them to be sold,
what can you do about it? The problem is of course
particularly acute because the parallel importer
will invariably be buying your goods in a country
where the price is lower, and selling at a discount
in a country where the price is higher, thus under-
cutting the prices of you or your exclusive licensee for that country.

On the one hand, why shouldn't a parallel importer
be able to do this? After all, the free movement of
goods is one of the fundamental principles of EC
competition law. But on the other hand, you as
trade mark owner should be able to protect your
brand image by having control over the quality of

the goods to which your trade mark is applied. There is therefore an obvious tension between competition law and intellectual property law. The compromise is what is known as 'the doctrine of exhaustion of rights'.

What the doctrine says is that you as trade mark owner cannot object to the use of your trade mark in relation to goods that have already been put on the market in the European Economic Area (EEA) by you or with your consent. In those circumstances, your trade mark rights are said to be exhausted. Importantly, you do, however, have a right to first market any particular consignment of your trade marked goods in the EEA; and it will be an infringement of your trade mark if a third party imports, sells or offers for sale a consignment of your trade marked goods which have not previously been marketed by you or with your consent in the EEA. For ease of reference, the EEA countries are: Austria, Belgium, Cyprus, Czech Republic, Denmark, Estonia, Finland, France, Germany, Greece, Hungary, Iceland, Ireland, Italy, Latvia, Liechtenstein, Lithuania, Luxembourg, Malta, Netherlands, Norway, Poland, Portugal, Slovak Republic, Slovenia, Spain, Sweden, Switzerland and the United Kingdom. Bulgaria and Romania are due to join on 1 January 2007.

The good news is that your consent to any particular consignment of your trade marked goods being put on the market in the EEA must be unequivocally demonstrated. This means that it is very difficult for parallel importers to argue that you have impliedly consented to your goods being imported into the EEA. In practice, to be certain of avoiding trade mark infringement proceedings, a parallel importer has to be able to establish the provenance of his goods and that they had originally been put on the market in the EEA by you or your licensee. This is a heavy burden and involves tracing the chain of supply into the EEA all the way back to you. Otherwise, you will have a trade mark infringement claim against the parallel importer.

There are nonetheless certain brand protection steps that you can take to protect against the difficulty of parallel imports:

- Make it clear to your licensees, in their contracts, that they can sell your trade marked goods only in their particular territories. If their territories are outside the EEA, you should stipulate in their contracts that your licensees cannot import goods into the EEA.
- Clearly mark your non-EEA goods and their packaging with a statement that they are 'not for resale within the EEA'.
- Apply a unique code to your trade marked goods and packaging so that you can identify the licensee and territory to whom you first sold

them. This will provide invaluable evidence as to whether or not you had originally consented to their sale in the EEA.

Even if your trade marked goods have been put on the market in the EEA by you or with your consent, you can still bring trade mark infringement proceedings against a parallel importer where you have a 'legitimate reason' for opposing importation (e.g. where the condition of your goods has been changed or impaired after you put them on the market). The 'legitimate reason' principle is invoked most frequently by trade mark owners in the context of the repackaging or relabelling of pharmaceuticals by parallel importers. In that context, there is again good news for you as brand owner, because the parallel importer must give you reasonable notice (e.g. 15 working days) that the repackaged or relabelled product is about to be sold, in order to give you time to react to and make objections to the intended packaging or labelling. You cannot, however, oppose repackaging or relabelling where to do so would be anti-competitive and deny the importer effective access to your market: this is a complex area upon which specific advice should be sought.

The general message therefore is that you do not have to tolerate parallel imports and may often be able to prevent them by means of trade mark infringement proceedings.

COPYRIGHT

As the owner of copyright in a work, you have the exclusive right to do and to authorise certain things to be done in relation to your work, namely:

- to copy the work
- to issue copies of the work to the public
- to rent or lend the work to the public
- to perform, show or play the work in public
- to communicate the work to the public
- to make an adaptation of the work or do any of the above in relation to an adaptation

A third party will infringe the copyright in your work if, without a licence from you, the third party does or authorises someone else to do any of the above acts.

Acts of civil infringement

Your copyright will be infringed if, without your permission, someone else:

- *Copies your work*: most people are broadly aware that you can't plagiarise someone else's work. It is a popular misconception, however, that you can copy someone else's work as long as you acknowledge and credit them as the author. In fact, copyright in a literary, dramatic, musical or artistic work is infringed by substantially reproducing the work in any material form, including electronically, without the author's permission. Acknowledging the author is irrelevant unless you have his permission or can rely upon one of the limited fair dealing defences. In order for your copyright in, for example, an artistic work to be infringed, the infringer must copy the whole or a substantial part of your work. What is regarded as 'substantial' is a question of fact and the test is more of a qualitative than a quantitative one. While the more that is taken increases the likelihood that a substantial part has been copied, quantity is not conclusive and if someone copies a small but significant part of your copyright work, they may still infringe the copyright in the work as a whole. The two works are compared and the court asks itself whether the allegedly infringing work incorporates a substantial part of the skill and labour expended by you in creating your copyright work. It is largely a question of impression.

- *Issues copies of your work to the public*: it will be an infringement of copyright to put into circulation copyright works which have not previously been put into circulation in the European Economic Area by you or with your consent.
- *Rents or lends copies of your work to the public* in relation to literary, dramatic and musical

works and certain types of artistic work, films
or sound recordings.

- *Performs, shows or plays your literary, dramatic
  or musical work in public*: performance includes
  the delivery of lectures, addresses, speeches and
  sermons and includes any mode of visual or
  acoustic presentation, including presentation
  by means of a sound recording, film or broadcast of the work.

- *Communicates your work to the public*: this is
  an act restricted by the copyright in a literary,
  dramatic, musical or artistic work, a sound
  recording, film or a broadcast. Communication
  to the public includes communication to the
  public by electronic transmission such as the
  broadcasting of the work.

- *Makes an adaptation of your work* or does any
  of the above acts in relation to an adaptation.
  This restriction only applies to literary, dramatic
  and musical works, but not to artistic works.

In order for someone to infringe copyright in
your work, the infringing work must have been
derived from your original copyright work,
whether directly or indirectly. In practice, you
need to establish a causal link, either that the
infringer did have access to and copied your work
or that the two works are so objectively similar
that the infringer must have had access to your
work and that the similarities are more likely to
be the result of copying than of coincidence.

There are also other secondary instances in which your copyright can be infringed. Broadly speaking, secondary infringers are those who do not themselves copy or authorise others to copy, but who instead deal commercially with infringing copies or articles. For example, if someone, without a licence from you, imports into the UK an article that he knows or believes to be an infringing copy, or possesses or deals with an article that he knows or believes to be an infringing copy, he will be committing a secondary infringement even though he himself was not responsible for the act of copying.

Defences to civil copyright infringement

If you find yourself on the receiving end of a claim for copyright infringement, there are certain defences which may be available to you. These are:

- the copyright owner consented to your use of the work (i.e. you have a licence, express or implied, to use it)
- you created the work independently and did not copy another work
- your use does not, qualitatively or quantitatively, amount to a substantial reproduction of the original copyright work

- you used a literary, dramatic, musical or artistic work fairly for the purposes of private study or research for a non-commercial purpose
- you used the work fairly for the purpose of criticism or review and news reporting
- you incidentally included the copyright material in an artistic work, sound recording, film or broadcast

Criminal copyright offences

As an alternative to civil proceedings, you might want to report a copyright infringer to Trading Standards who may decide to prosecute the infringer criminally and who also have powers to execute search warrants. Although this may be a more cost effective means of dealing with infringers because the cost of the prosecution is borne by the state rather than by you as the brand owner, the disadvantages are that: you lose control of the action; there is no guarantee that Trading Standards will elect to prosecute; you will not receive any compensation from criminal proceedings although the infringer may be subject to a penalty or imprisonment.

Criminal copyright offences are targeted at those who know or have reason to believe that they are making or dealing with pirated copies of your copyright work. Generally, a person will be guilty of a criminal offence if he, without a licence from you:

- makes for sale or hire
- imports into the UK (other than for private or domestic use)
- possesses in the course of a business with a view to committing any act infringing the copyright
- in the course of business:
  - sells or lets for hire
  - offers or exposes for sale or hire
  - exhibits in public
  - distributes
- distributes otherwise than in the course of business to such an extent as to affect you prejudicially as the owner of the copyright

an article which he knows or has reason to believe is an infringing copy of a copyright work.

There are other criminal copyright offences relating to equipment used to facilitate copyright infringements. For example, a criminal offence will be committed if a person makes or has in his possession an article which is specially designed or adapted for making infringing copies of your copyright work if he knew or had reason to believe that it was to be used to make infringing copies for sale or hire or for use in the course of business.

DESIGNS
UK registered designs

Infringement

If you are the proprietor of a UK registered design, you have the exclusive right to use and to authorise third parties to use (a) your design and (b) any other design which does not produce a different overall impression than your design on an informed user. Broadly, an informed user means a person who is familiar with the particular sector to which the design applies. Such use includes:

- making
- offering
- putting on the market
- importing
- exporting
- using
- stocking

any product which either incorporates your design or to which your design is applied.

A third party will infringe your UK registered design if it carries out any of the above acts without your consent. Note that the third party does not necessarily have to copy your registered design in order to infringe it.

Defences

Your UK registered design will *not* be infringed where the third party:

- has your consent to use the design
- uses a design that creates a different overall impression to your design in the eyes of an informed user
- is successful in invalidating your registered design
- makes use of your design:
  - for private and non-commercial purposes, including any experiments
  - for teaching purposes (such use must not unduly prejudice the exploitation of your design and must acknowledge the source)
  - in a component part used for the repair of a complex product in order to restore its original appearance

Even if a third party is guilty of infringing your UK registered design, it will not be liable to pay you damages if it can prove that it was not aware and had no reasonable ground for supposing that your design was registered. To defeat this 'innocent infringement' defence, you as registered proprietor should make sure that any product incorporating your design or to which your design is applied is marked clearly with the words 'registered design' and the registered number of the design.

UK unregistered designs

Infringement

UK unregistered design right carries with it the exclusive right to make articles to the design or to make a design document recording the design in order to enable such articles to be made.

Due to the overlap between copyright and design right, the unregistered design infringement rules are very complicated and the question as to which one of your rights is being infringed will depend upon whether the infringer is copying your article alone or copying your underlying design drawing with a view to making your article.

If a third party 'reverse-engineers' your article by reproducing or authorising another person to reproduce your design by making articles exactly or substantially to that design, then it will normally be a primary infringement of your design right.

In limited circumstances, your article will attract both design right and copyright protection, but you can't claim for infringement of both. Copyright takes precedence; so if something infringes your copyright, it can't also infringe your design right. If therefore your article (i.e. the end product rather than just the design drawing of it) is itself an artistic work, then making articles exactly or substantially to your design will be copyright rather than design right infringement. However, it is not very often that your industrial or commercial design will be of sufficient artistic craftsmanship for the article itself to attract copyright protection, so making articles exactly or substantially to your design will more frequently be a design right rather than a copyright infringement.

So far, I have been considering a third party who makes an *article* to your design. If, however, a third party does not make an article but rather copies your design *drawing* for the purpose of enabling articles to be made to the design, that will infringe your copyright rather than your design right in the design drawing.

In summary, while reproduction by a third party of your two-dimensional drawing embodying your design is a breach of your copyright in that drawing, making a three-dimensional article to that design will be a breach of your design right (unless your article is itself an artistic work, in which case it will instead be a breach of your copyright).

The above acts are all primary infringements. It is also possible for a third party, who does not himself copy or authorise the copying of your design but instead deals commercially with infringing articles, to be a secondary infringer if, without your consent, he:

- imports (or proposes to import) into the UK
- has in his possession in the UK for commercial purposes
- sells, lets or offers for sale or hire in the course of a business

an article which is and which the third party has reason to believe is an infringing article.

Defences

Your UK unregistered design right will *not* be infringed where the third party:

- has your consent to use the design
- has not reproduced exactly or substantially your unregistered design
- has not used its article for commercial purposes and/or in the course of a business, i.e. has used it for private or non-commercial purposes (this defence only applies in cases of secondary infringement)

Even if a third party is guilty of infringing your UK unregistered design, it will not be liable to pay you damages as a result if it can prove that it was not aware or had no reason to believe that design right subsisted in the design.

Compulsory licensing of your unregistered design

If a third party infringes your UK unregistered design during the last five years of its protection, the third party can undertake to enter into a licence (known as a 'licence of right') with you to use the design in order to avoid injunctive relief and to limit any damages. This might seem unpalatable to you considering that your design is still protected by design right, but any third party is allowed to apply to the Patent Office for a compulsory licence from you during the last five years of protection of your unregistered design and you are compelled by statute to grant that licence to the third party. It is not quite as bad as it sounds though, because you are able to negotiate the licence on commercial terms. However, if you are unable to agree terms with the licensee, then terms will be settled by the Comptroller at the Patent Office.

Community designs (registered and unregistered)

A third party can only infringe your unregistered community design if the design is copied by the third party; so there will be no infringement if the third party creates an independent work without reference to your design. On that basis, unregistered community design protection does not operate unless your design has been made available to the public as it would not otherwise be available for a third party to copy. Even if your design has been made available to the public, it is a defence for a third party to show that it is reasonable to assume that it was not familiar with your design.

Community registered designs can be infringed without proving copying if a similar design is adopted.

You are not subject to compulsory licensing in the last five years of your community design, whether registered or unregistered.

Criminal offences

There are no criminal sanctions against third parties in relation to infringement of your registered or unregistered designs.

You should, however, be aware that claiming an article to be a 'registered design' when it is not is a criminal offence. It is also a criminal offence knowingly to register a design that you know to be invalid.

Chapter

8

. . . .

ENFORCING YOUR IP AND THE REMEDIES AVAILABLE TO YOU

Soldiers find wars, and lawyers find out still Litigious men.

John Donne, *The Canonisation*

HOW TO REACT TO AN INFRINGEMENT OF YOUR RIGHTS

Having gone to the trouble and expense of registering your trade marks or creating your copyright works or designs, you must ensure that you are vigilant in policing and enforcing such valuable assets.

Do you have a clear reporting procedure and chain of command?

It is important to have in place a clear chain of command and reporting procedure. All employees, from secretaries to the board of directors, should know to whom within your organisation to report a suspected infringement. Who has responsibility for particular brands? Who has authority to instruct external counsel? Who has authority to decide whether or not to sue?

Your distributors and/or licensees should be required, as a term of your contract with them, to notify you immediately as and when they learn of a third party who is potentially infringing your IP rights.

If you see infringing goods on the market, take photographs of them or make sample purchases and retain your receipts.

The need for speed

Any failure to take immediate action against potential infringers could jeopardise your prospects of success in any legal action. One of the remedies available for an infringement of your IP rights is an interim injunction (see page 163). An injunction is an order of the court which prevents any further infringement. Interim injunctions are granted on an urgent basis as soon as it is discovered that a potential infringement is taking place. Any delay in applying for an interim injunction can be fatal and can mean that the injunction is not ultimately granted. It is therefore crucial that you react immediately to potential infringements, particularly where the competing product has not yet been launched, hence the need for employees, distributors and licensees to notify you as soon as they become aware of a potential infringement. As soon as you do become aware of a potential infringement, you should consult external counsel without delay.

The importance of a confusion log

In the case of third parties using names or marks similar to your registered or unregistered trade marks, your employees (e.g. particularly telephone operators), distributors and licensees should all be notified of the problem and given instructions to keep records (e.g. e-mails, letters, contemporaneous notes of telephone conversations) of any evidence that indicates that a likelihood of confusion has arisen. Such confusion could include any of the following:

- consumers mistakenly contacting you to complain about/comment upon the competing product or its advertising and merchandising
- the media mistakenly contacting you to ask about the competing product in the belief that it is your product
- press/television/radio mistakenly contacting you in respect of advertisements for the competing product which they believe to have been placed with them by you
- the industry mistakenly contacting you for orders/queries in respect of the competing product
- supermarkets/stores mistakenly contacting you for orders/queries in respect of the competing product

In such cases, a contemporaneous note should be kept detailing the name and address of the person confused, the date and the nature of the confusion. Such records will provide an invaluable database of potential witnesses for external counsel in respect of any trade mark infringement or passing off proceedings which you commence.

Cease and desist letters

Rather than rushing straight into suing a third party infringer, the English courts expect IP owners to follow a reasonable and proportionate procedure by first writing to the infringer to give full details of your claim. Failure to send a claim letter can result in adverse costs consequences at a later date.

Your letter of claim should:

- give concise details of the rights that you own and your complaint, to enable the recipient to understand and investigate the claim
- enclose copies of the essential documents upon which you rely (e.g. your trade mark/registered design certificates or copyright works; any evidence of infringement)
- identify and ask for copies of any essential documents which you wish to see
- ask for a prompt acknowledgement, followed by a full written response within a reasonable stated period (e.g. 21 days)
- state whether court proceedings will be issued if a satisfactory response is not received within the stated period
- state if you wish to enter into a mediation or any other method of alternative dispute resolution (see page 159)

For blatant infringements of your IP rights, a strongly worded cease and desist letter prepared by external counsel will hopefully secure undertakings from the infringer to cease its infringing activities. Such a letter should be sent as soon as possible after discovery of the potential infringement of your IP rights.

If the cease and desist letter is ignored or does not provide a satisfactory response, you should seek advice from external counsel as to the merits and costs of suing for infringement of your rights.

In urgent cases, you might not have time for a cease and desist letter and it may be that you have to rush off and apply for an injunction without delay and without even notifying the infringer.

A word of warning about making unjustified threats

You need to exercise caution when making threats of trade mark, UK registered design, UK design right and patent infringement proceedings against those down the supply chain, such as wholesalers, retailers and distributors.

If your threat is deemed to be unjustifiable, then the person threatened will have a self-standing cause of action (often referred to as a 'threats action') against you and could sue you for damages. For this reason, whenever making threats of proceedings it is sensible to get advance legal clearance.

The test as to what constitutes a threat is very broad and any hint at bringing proceedings may be deemed to be a threat. However, the mere notification to a third party that your trade mark is registered will not be a threat.

Threats actions cannot be brought in respect of threatened claims for copyright or database right infringement.

Website infringements and service providers

If a third party is committing infringing acts via the internet (e.g. selling counterfeit/unlicensed goods or goods that infringe your copyright/ designs on its website), you may want to consider writing not only to the third party operating the website but also to the internet service provider or the host of the website (e.g. eBay).

In the case of copyright infringements, the High Court has a specific power to grant an injunction (see page 162) against a service provider where the service provider has actual knowledge of someone using that service to infringe copyright.

Although there is no equivalent statutory power to grant injunctions against service providers for other IP infringements, under common law a brand owner may be entitled to an injunction against the service provider or website host if the website contains infringing content. As a matter of practice a service provider or website host will, upon receipt of a cease and desist letter, often take immediate steps to withdraw any goods being offered on its website that are alleged to be infringing goods, while it conducts further investigations.

Contacting the service provider can therefore be a speedy way of dealing with website infringements, but as explained above, beware unjustified threats.

You should bear in mind that the availability of infringing goods on the internet (which can of course be accessed worldwide) does not mean that an infringement of your IP rights is being committed worldwide. The English courts require the website to be directed in some way towards the English market (e.g. online orders can be placed in sterling; the website provides for shipment to the UK; the underlying company operating the website is based in the UK; the underlying business is carried out from the UK; advertising is directed at and takes place in the UK).

What next?

If the letter of claim does not produce the desired result and the infringer refuses to cease its infringing activities, or if you are otherwise unable to resolve the dispute on a commercial basis, you have four alternatives:

- sue
- pursue a form of alternative dispute resolution
- seek to persuade Trading Standards to bring a criminal IP prosecution (see page 118)
- give up!

Commencing proceedings

Intellectual property cases are dealt with by specialist intellectual property judges in the Chancery Division of the High Court (based in London).

You will no longer hear lawyers talking about 'writs', as they are now called 'claim forms'. The claim form is a court document which sets out brief details of the nature and value of your claim and the remedies that you are seeking. In order to get a claim up and running, the claim form must be 'issued' in the High Court upon payment of a fixed fee. Within a short time after, or at the same time as, service of the claim form, you must serve your particulars of claim.

The particulars of claim set out the full nature of your complaint: who you are; who the defendant is; what rights you own; the factual background relating to your complaint; the nature of the defendant's infringing activity; and the remedies that you are seeking.

In brief, the next stages of the litigation are as follows: the defendant serves its defence; you then have an opportunity to serve any reply you may have to the defence; there is then a case management conference at the court when the court gives directions on the future conduct of the case; the parties then exchange documentary evidence (a process known as 'disclosure'); they then exchange written statements of witnesses of fact, followed by any expert reports; the case then proceeds to trial. The whole process, from issue of claim form to trial, takes in the region of 9 to 18 months.

Claim forms, particulars of claim, the defence and any reply are open to public inspection at the High Court so the press may pick up on the existence and substance of your claim. Where the details of your claim are sensitive or confidential you can apply for a confidentiality order.

The good news is that if you are successful, not only will you receive a compensation award from the court (see page 171) but the defendant will also be ordered to pay your reasonable legal costs of the litigation. The flipside, however, is that if you are unsuccessful, you will be ordered to pay the defendant's reasonable costs of the litigation.

Alternative dispute resolution (ADR)

ADR is simply a form of dispute resolution other than court litigation. A distinction needs to be drawn between methods of dispute resolution which involve a binding determination by a third party (which include arbitration, expert determination, adjudication and normal litigation) and those which do not. These other forms of dispute resolution require the parties, albeit with third party assistance, to reach a settlement themselves. Such forms of assisted settlement include the following:

- *Mediation*: a mutual third party (usually a barrister or senior solicitor) is appointed to help you and the other side to reach a negotiated settlement. There are no fixed rules for the procedure that a mediation should follow. Following a brief initial presentation of your and the other side's case in front of the mediator, the process then involves 'shuttle diplomacy' by the mediator who expands on and explores the parties' positions with a view to promoting a settlement. This is the most common form of

ADR for IP cases, particularly as the UK Patent Office provides its own mediation service where any type of IP dispute can be mediated by a member of its Mediation Service Team who has specific experience of IP hearings. Such mediations take place at the Patent Office's London or Newport offices.

- *Mini trial*: this is a more formal type of mediation which is structured more like a court hearing and usually involves legal presentations to a panel of senior directors of each party with a neutral chairman. After the presentations, the executives attempt to negotiate a settlement based on what they have heard.
- *Early neutral evaluation/appraisal*: you and the other side send your submissions to an independent third party, often a judge or senior lawyer, who will then provide his view on the likely outcome.

Trading Standards

See page 118 for an explanation of the cheaper option of seeking to persuade Trading Standards to investigate a criminal prosecution against the infringer.

Give up!

Naturally, you may not want, in all cases, to incur the cost of litigation. Different levels of infringement will call for different responses from you the brand owner.

One factor that may be relevant in your decision as to whether to keep pursuing the infringer is the position that the infringer occupies in the supply chain. You may be more inclined to pursue large-scale manufacturers and distributors than small-scale retailers.

REMEDIES

If your IP rights have been infringed, there are generally six potential remedies available to you:

- an injunction: a temporary or permanent order against the defendant to stop infringing your rights
- an interim order that the continuation of the defendant's activities be subject to the lodging of guarantees
- delivery up, recall, seizure or destruction of the infringing goods/advertising and promotional materials
- compensation: either by way of damages for the loss you have suffered or payment to you of the profits the defendant has made from its infringing activities
- disclosure of the identity and whereabouts of other wrongdoers in the distribution network

and information/documentation on infringing
products
- publication of judicial decisions

Injunctions

What is an injunction?

Most people have heard of an injunction, although
there are a number of misconceptions about what
it is and how it is obtained. It takes the form of
an order of the court, either compelling the defendant to do something (*mandatory injunction*) or
prohibiting the defendant from doing something
(*prohibitive injunction*). So in the case of an
infringement of your IP rights, you could, for
example, obtain a mandatory injunction compelling a competitor to take down signage which
reproduces your copyright work, or a prohibitive
injunction preventing a retailer from selling products bearing a sign which resembles your trade
mark.

Two forms of injunction are available depending
on when, during the course of proceedings, you
apply for them:

- *Interim injunction*: this is an injunction granted
  before there has been a full trial of the case on

the merits, and usually at a very early stage (e.g. as soon as you discover there has been an infringement of your rights). It is a temporary and urgent remedy, which only lasts until the trial.

- *Permanent injunction*: this is an injunction which is granted at the trial, after the court has heard the case and reached a decision on the merits. It is a final remedy which applies forever, e.g. to prevent the defendant infringing your trade mark in the manner about which you made a complaint. A permanent injunction will only be granted where there is clear evidence that the defendant will continue to infringe.

Breach of an injunction amounts to contempt of court, which can in turn lead to imprisonment.

Special considerations for interim injunctions

An interim injunction is a remedy which can nip in the bud any infringements of your IP rights. It is therefore a very important weapon in the armoury of a brand owner. However, it is a draconian remedy and as such is a discretionary form of relief and only ordered by the court where it is really necessary to ensure that justice is done. The court will be alive to attempts by brand owners to obtain interim injunctions in order to obtain commercial advantage or to inconvenience the defendant. You must therefore satisfy the following criteria in order to obtain an interim injunction:

- You must have a genuine underlying legal complaint. You cannot apply for an injunction other than as an adjunct to proceedings for infringement of a legal right. The grant of an interim injunction normally signals the beginning of an action for, for example, infringement of your copyright or trade mark.
- The activity which is the subject of your complaint must be something where you can only be protected by the grant of an immediate injunction, and where you could not be compensated in some other way, for example by a subsequent award of damages. If the court believes that an award of damages could adequately compensate you for any arguable infringement of your rights, then it will not grant an injunction but will leave you to pursue your remedy for damages. In the case of trade mark infringement, it will often be self-evident that damages will not be an adequate remedy because of the untold damage to the brand that could result from a third party using your trade mark without permission.
- The court will always look at the whole picture and will try to assess whether, in the short

term, it is fairer to grant you an interim injunction (bearing in mind the loss, damage and inconvenience that will be caused to the defendant) than it is to allow the defendant to continue with the activity which is thought to be an infringement (bearing in mind the loss, damage and inconvenience that this will cause to you) until the full trial takes place. This is what is known as the 'balance of convenience' test. It is generally more difficult to obtain an interim injunction to prevent something which has already started than it is to prevent something which is just about to happen. Therefore, if you discover an infringement of your IP rights, at say a trade fair, before the infringing product has been launched, your prospects of obtaining an interim injunction will be higher if you move immediately.

- You must move very quickly, as soon as you become aware of the potential infringement. A delay, even of a few days, can sometimes be fatal, hence the need for speed referred to at page 151. An injunction can be obtained extremely quickly (within three to four days of instructing external counsel and, in extreme cases, within hours) if this will prevent an infringement of your rights.

- You must give what is called a 'cross undertaking in damages'. This is an undertaking that you give to the court that if you are granted your interim injunction, but after the full trial the court decides that it ought not to have been granted, then you will compensate the defendant for all of its loss and damage suffered as a result of being restrained by the injunction up until the full trial. The cross undertaking in damages can be onerous and you should always seek advice from external counsel before providing it.

You can go to court without giving the defendant any, or much, notice, particularly where you have only just discovered the infringement (or threatened infringement) and where the defendant is just about to do something which could be prevented if an injunction were granted quickly.

At the interim stage, the court generally will not be able to decide definitively whether or not your IP rights have been infringed. That question will be determined at full trial which normally takes place within 9 to 18 months from commencement of proceedings. At the interim injunction stage the court is only deciding whether or not you have a serious argument that your rights are being (or are about to be) infringed; and that it is fairer to grant you an interim injunction until the final trial takes place than it is to allow the defendant to continue with its activities until the trial takes place.

Two extreme forms of injunction, which may be available for an infringement of your IP rights, without notifying the defendant, are 'freezing injunctions' (to freeze an infringer's assets to ensure that they are not dissipated prior to any damages award) and 'search orders' (requiring the infringer to allow your solicitors to search for and seize evidence of infringement which you fear might otherwise be destroyed).

Be prepared . . .

For the cost: interim injunction applications can be time consuming and expensive. They are not obtained merely by filling out forms. External counsel has to prepare detailed witness statements and collate key documents in order to be able to apply for an interim injunction on your behalf. Because of the cost generally and the additional exposure created by the cross undertaking in damages, you should think seriously before embarking upon an application for an interim injunction.

With all relevant factual information: because of the need to move very quickly, help external counsel by presenting them with the following background evidence in as orderly a fashion as possible:

- details as to your ownership of the relevant IP right
- the importance of the IP right to you, e.g. costs involved in developing it, advertising expense, media schedule, reputation and goodwill evidence (e.g. industry awards, press coverage, copy advertisements)
- a chronology detailing how/when you discovered the potentially infringing use
- any evidence of the infringing activity (e.g. photographs, sample purchases)
- any confusion evidence, e.g. confusion log (see page 151)
- your latest accounts (for the cross undertaking in damages)

For the unexpected: because of the speed with which interim injunctions are applied for, and the fact that the court only has the opportunity to look in a fairly cursory way at the evidence, applications for interim injunctions can be unpredictable.

Order for the lodging of guarantees

As an alternative to an interim injunction, the court may decide to allow the alleged infringing activities of the defendant to continue pending trial but subject to the lodging of certain guarantees by the defendant that he will compensate you if those activities are found to be infringing at trial.

Delivery up, recall, seizure and destruction

Delivery up

The court has power to order an infringer to deliver up, to you as the rights owner, any goods, materials or articles which the infringer has in his possession, custody or control in the course of business and which:

- infringe your registered (or unregistered) trade mark
- are infringing copies of your copyright work
- are specifically designed or adapted for making copies of your copyright work
- infringe your registered design or unregistered design right
- are specifically designed or adapted for making articles to your unregistered design provided that the infringer has knowledge or reason to believe that it has been or will be used to make an infringing article

A delivery up order is normally made to enable the infringing goods, materials or articles to be destroyed or forfeited (see below).

Recall from channels of commerce

The court may order that appropriate measures be carried out, at the expense of the infringer, to recall from channels of commerce (1) infringing goods and (2) materials and implements principally used in the creation or manufacture of infringing goods.

Seizure of infringing copies

This self-help remedy for copyright infringements only is rarely used and has considerable limitations. In practice, it is only ever used against Del Trotter-type street traders trading out of suitcases.

Technically, you as copyright owner (or a person authorised by you) are entitled to seize and detain any infringing copies which you find being offered for sale or hire. But the limitations to this remedy are as follows:

- you must give advance notice of the time and place of your proposed seizure to your local police station
- you may enter only premises to which the public has access
- you may not seize anything from the infringer's permanent or regular place of business
- you may not use force
- you must leave, at the place where the infringing copies were seized, a notice in a prescribed form

Destruction

Once infringing goods, materials or articles have been delivered up to you as rights owner pursuant to a court order, you can then make an application to the court that they be destroyed or forfeited to such person as the court may think fit.

As with injunctions, no order for destruction will be made if damages would be an adequate remedy.

Damages/Account of profits

Compensation is the usual remedy for an infringement of your IP rights, unless you can justify the need for an injunction or delivery up/destruction.

The traditional position was that your compensation could take one of two forms, which you had to elect (you could not have both):

• damages
• an account of profits

However, under the IP Enforcement Directive, as bought into force in the UK by the IP Enforcement Regulations in April 2006, where the defendant knows, or has reasonable grounds to know, that he is engaging in infringing activity, the court must take into account all appropriate aspects in compensating you for the 'actual prejudice' you have suffered. This includes both your lost profits and any unfair profits made by the defendant, plus any 'moral prejudice' you may have suffered. As a result, although this has not yet been tested in the English courts, an election between damages or an account of profits may no longer be necessary in these circumstances.

The purpose of a damages award is to put you in the same financial position that you would have been in had the infringement not been committed. Depending upon the nature of your right which has been infringed and the facts of the case, a court will normally employ one of two alternative methods to quantify your loss:

- calculate a reasonable licence fee or royalty which you might have charged the infringer had he sought your consent to use your IP
- calculate the lost sales revenue, and therefore lost profits, which you have suffered as a result of the infringing goods competing with yours

In certain circumstances, you may be able to claim for other heads of loss in addition to reasonable licence fee/lost sales revenue:

- loss of reputation/brand image, for example where an infringing product is inferior to yours and therefore injures your reputation

- dilution or erosion of your goodwill or brand name
- loss of opportunity to license your IP elsewhere
- additional damages for flagrant breach of your copyright or your unregistered design right
- so-called 'moral prejudice'

The court will make certain deductions from your damages award as follows:

- Operating costs which you would have had to incur in order to earn the licence fee/sales revenue.
- To mitigate your loss: in the context of damages claims generally, you must take all reasonable steps to try to limit the loss you have suffered. This is often referred to as 'mitigation' by lawyers. The basic position is that you cannot recover damages in respect of a loss that you could have avoided. In the case of infringements of intellectual property rights, mitigation is less of a problem given that there is often no obvious way for you to try to reduce your loss.

The alternative to a damages award is to seek an account of the defendant's profits, the aim of which is to make the defendant hand over all profits made from his infringing activities. If the defendant's volume of sales is very high, this may provide you with more compensation than damages assessed by reference to your likely lost profits. You are not, however, automatically entitled to an account of profits as it is a discretionary remedy. In practice, an account of profits is rarely sought due to the difficulties experienced and complex expert evidence required to determine which of the defendant's profits are legitimate and which have been made as a result of the infringement.

Disclosure of the identity and whereabouts of other wrongdoers and information on infringing products

Often you will want to trace infringing activity all the way up the supply chain. You can compel, via the courts, any of the following people to disclose information and documentation relating to the identity and whereabouts of other infringers (e.g. producers, manufacturers, suppliers, retailers and wholesalers of infringing goods) and the quantities of infringing goods produced, manufactured, delivered, received or ordered (as well as the price obtained):

- a defendant whom you have successfully sued for infringement of your IP rights
- a potential defendant who is likely to be a party to subsequent proceedings

- a person who has inadvertently or intentionally become mixed up in infringing activity and who holds information which will assist you (known as a 'Norwich Pharmacal' Order)

Publication of judicial decisions

The court may order that appropriate measures be taken, at the expense of the infringer, for the dissemination of information concerning the court decision, including displaying the judgement and publishing it (e.g. via prominent advertising) in full or in part.

Chapter

9

....

HOW TO AVOID INFRINGING OTHER PEOPLE'S IP

It is all very well to copy what you see; it is much better to draw what you see only in memory.

Edgar Degas

HOW TO AVOID INFRINGING OTHER PEOPLE'S IP

Equally important to protecting your own IP is ensuring that you do not inadvertently infringe the IP rights of someone else. The last thing you want to happen is for you to launch your new product which has been years in developing, or your sexy (and expensive) new advertising campaign, only to receive a claim that it infringes someone else's trade marks, copyright and designs.

You should bear in mind that for civil trade mark infringement and passing off, you do not have to intend to infringe someone else's rights. Even if you inadvertently use someone else's trade mark, distinctive name or get-up, you will be infringing. Equally, if you make or sell a product which, without your knowledge, is a UK or community registered design, you will infringe that design. The position is different for copyright and design right infringement where an element of copying is required.

This list of dos and don'ts should minimise the risk of you inadvertently infringing someone else's rights:

- *DO: understand.* Your product development, marketing and advertising teams (and agencies) all need to have a basic understanding of the different types of IP rights that exist, so that they appreciate how to avoid infringing someone else's IP. It is no good if only your in-house legal team know the problems and how to avoid them. Annual refresher presentations/workshops from in-house or external counsel are essential. Lending your commercial/creative people a copy of this book would be a good start!

- *DO: search the internet.* Before even conducting a trade mark, registered design or patent search, you should do your own internet searches to check any conflicts with your proposed new name, concept, product or packaging. You will be surprised at how many brand owners overlook such a basic research tool as an internet search engine. You may be able to discard your proposed name without incurring any solicitors' or trade mark agents' fees.

- *DO: always conduct a pre-emptive trade mark search* (see page 6) as soon as you have devised a new product name, brand name, business name, packaging, logo or advertising slogan. Not only will this tell you whether there is a risk of infringing existing trade marks, it will also tell you whether your proposed mark is available for registration and therefore worth proceeding with. Seeking legal approval the day before the launch is too late!

- *DO: always conduct a pre-emptive registered design/patent search* before developing a new product: again, this will confirm whether you need to worry about similar products and whether you can register your own product.

- *DO: conduct a company search.* If you are planning to use a new company or trading name, check that there are no conflicting company names already registered at Companies House. External counsel can conduct a quick and inexpensive search of the companies register for you.

- *DO: conduct a domain name search.* Regardless of whether you want to register your own domain name, conduct a domain name search to see if anyone else is using your proposed new company or trading name as their website address. For example, at www.netbenefit.com you can type in any name and the search engine will tell you which suffixes have already been registered to whom and which are still available.

- *DON'T: copy.* Using someone else's literary, dramatic, musical or artistic works without permission will amount to a copyright infringement. As can be seen from page 14, the threshold for copyright protection is very low and copyright can subsist in things as diverse as photographs, illustrations, design drawings, labels, text (e.g. from a competitor's brochure or website), music and slogans. Whenever using or reproducing such works, always check the copyright position first.

- *DON'T: use someone else's trade mark* without taking legal advice: you should ensure that any comparative advertising claims, or any reference to another's trade mark on your packaging, will not constitute a trade mark infringement.

- *DO: obtain copy clearance.* It is very easy to infringe someone else's copyright or trade marks unwittingly when producing product brochures and print or screen advertising. If you have any doubts or concerns, speak to external counsel to get legal approval.

- *DON'T: confuse.* You should not create confusion between your brand/products and competitors' products, trade marks, trade names, packaging or advertising. To do so could result in any one of a complaint to the Advertising Standards Authority, a complaint to Trading Standards, a claim for trade mark infringement and a claim for passing off.

- *DO: exercise care in your design briefs/advertising synopses and internal communications.* If you are specifically targeting a competitor or its products (e.g. a comparative advertising campaign or a competing product launch), always assume that internal documents (meeting notes, board minutes, internal memoranda, e-mails, marketing proposals, design briefs, manuscript notes) could ultimately be seen by the court in any infringement proceedings. An e-mail from your managing director to your commercial director saying 'Let's rip off their look and feel and tie the bastards up in legal fees for years' is not a helpful document to have to disclose to the court.

Chapter

10

. . . .

REGISTERING AND PROTECTING YOUR DOMAIN NAMES

There is very little music in the name of Jack, if any at all, indeed. It does not thrill. It produces absolutely no vibrations.

Oscar Wilde, *The Importance of Being Earnest*

DOMAIN NAMES

What is a domain name?

A domain name is a name by which a company, organisation or person is known on the internet. Only one person can own any particular domain name, so it is effectively an exclusive address on the worldwide web.

What is the value of a domain name?

In our increasingly e-literate world, the commercial value of domain names is significant. Domain names have become distinctive brands in themselves, lastminute.com and amazon.com being two of the most successful. Although the dot com boom has now passed, domain names remain valuable commodities and you should regard them as part of your brand portfolio.

Registering a domain name

If you have not already registered a domain name for your business, it is possible to do so via a number of registration websites such as netbenefit.com or register.com. Using a WHOIS search, you can conduct an availability search against suffixes and name combinations. Global suffixes (gTLDs) – .com, .org, .biz and .info – are available to anyone in the world, while country-code suffixes (ccTLDs) – .org.uk and .co.uk – are only available to users in that particular country. Available domain names may be registered for a small annual fee and must be renewed after the initial minimum term of two years or else they will lapse.

Problems with the registration system

Domain names are allocated on a 'first come, first served' basis. The problem with this is that the allocating bodies only check whether the exact domain name somebody wants to register has already been registered. If it has not, that person can register it by providing name and address details – which are not checked and could be (and often are) bogus – and paying the registration fee. There is no requirement to show any pre-existing trade mark rights or interest in the domain name. This has a number of consequences:

- If you are registering a domain name, you should check that the name is not already a registered trade mark. Although you may be allowed to register the domain name, the use of that domain name could constitute trade mark infringement or passing off.

- As a brand owner you may wish to register a portfolio of domain names to ensure both that customers are directed to your business whatever related web address they type in, and that competitors or individuals acting in bad faith (known as 'cybersquatters') do not take unfair advantage of your goodwill by registering domain names incorporating, or similar to, your trade mark. On the other hand, you may decide that registering .com and .co.uk should cover anyone who is likely to want to find your website and that it is not necessary to register say .org and .eu for every possible combination of variants of your name.
- You should monitor any use of domain names similar to your domain names and trade marks, via regular WHOIS searches. Actively managing and protecting your domain name portfolio is a crucial part of modern brand strategy.

Where bogus details as to the registrant of the offending domain name are revealed by a WHOIS search, there are still other options available to you. You may be able to determine the identity of the registrant by contacting the domain name registry or the internet service provider, and if they are unwilling to disclose the identity you can apply to court for an order compelling them to do so (known as a 'Norwich Pharmacal' order: see page 175).

Disputes

Stopping a third party from using a domain name which you believe is infringing your trade mark or taking unfair advantage of your goodwill does not necessarily have to involve court proceedings. The first step will often be to write to the registered owner of the domain name (to the extent that they are identifiable) advising them of your rights and asking them to stop using the domain name. It is possible, but unlikely, that the registered owner may not have realised the domain name contained your trade mark and will agree to stop using it, usually subject to repayment of his registration expenses.

However, given the global nature of the internet and the fact that there is no division by industry sector, the third party owner may have an equally legitimate right to use the same domain name. For example, the domain name nissan.com was first registered by a company called Nissan Computer Corp in Raleigh, North Carolina. Because this company had a legitimate reason for choosing the domain name, the global giant Nissan Motor Company was unable to register the domain name. Similarly, although ritz.com takes you to the homepage of Ritz hotels, who is to say that the famous hotel brand should be more entitled to the domain name than Ritz cameras or Ritz crackers?

Sometimes, however, domain names incorporating well-known trade marks are registered by a cybersquatter with the deliberate purpose of blocking your use of that name, attracting internet users to their own site, or redirecting them to another site in return for linking fees, by taking advantage of the goodwill in that trade mark. Cybersquatters register hundreds of such domain names in the mistaken belief that they can sell the domain name to the trade mark owner at an inflated price. It is more than likely that such people will ignore your correspondence or try to demand a bounty for the domain name. In those circumstances a firmer approach will be required.

As the owner of a trade mark or goodwill which has been infringed by the registrant of an identical or similar domain name, you have two main forms of recourse in such situations: a civil court claim for trade mark infringement and/or passing off, or alternative dispute resolution via the ICANN/Nominet/EURid procedures.

Trade mark infringement/ passing off

As with any other claim for trade mark infringement or passing off, the usual requirements set out on pages 128–130 and 9–10 must be satisfied. These requirements are more onerous than those which much be satisfied to effect a compulsory transfer of the domain name under the dispute resolution procedure, but the advantage of a successful claim for trade mark infringement or passing off is that the court can grant an injunction to stop the owner from using the domain name immediately and can award you damages to compensate you for the damage to your trade mark, as well as ordering that the defendant should pay your reasonable legal costs.

The English courts have given cybersquatters a clear message that registering a well-known domain name as an 'instrument of fraud' to hold the brand owner to ransom or to sell it to a third party at a premium, or using the domain name to piggy-back on a brand owner's reputation, will not be tolerated.

You should consider registering your key domain names as trade marks to make such proceedings easier. For example, Macfarlanes has registered www.macfarlanes.com as a trade mark.

Alternative dispute resolution

A cheaper and sometimes quicker alternative means of dealing with domain name registrations which you object to is to follow the relevant dispute resolution procedure, albeit the only remedy they provide is the compulsory transfer, cancellation or amendment of the offending domain name. No compensation is available. The most utilised regulatory procedures are operated by the Internet Corporation for Assigned Names and Numbers (ICANN) (in the case of the gTLDs – .com, .net etc.) or Nominet (in the case of .uk domain names). Another important regulatory procedure is now that of the European Registry of Internet Domain Names (EURid) which is facilitated by the Prague-based Czech Arbitration Court and which handles disputes relating to .eu domain names.

Complaints to ICANN should be made in writing to the World Intellectual Property Organisation (WIPO), which will appoint an independent expert who will invite the owner of the domain name to respond and will then decide within about six weeks whether the registration was made in 'bad faith'. A fixed fee is payable.

Complaints to Nominet should be made direct in writing. Nominet will then try to mediate by telephone, which has had successful results, and will only require a fee if mediation with the domain name owner is unsuccessful, upon which an expert is appointed to decide within a similar period whether the registration was 'abusive'.

Complaints to EURid should be made in writing to the Czech Arbitration Court in hard and electronic forms. The Czech Arbitration Court will then forward that complaint to the respondent, who is allowed an opportunity to respond, following which the Court will appoint a single-member or three-member panel (at the claimant's election) to decide the dispute. A fixed fee is payable, the amount of which depends on the number of panellists.

In the majority of cases, dispute resolution will be the most effective procedure, particularly as multiple names can be recovered in a single action. However, it may not always be possible to avoid court proceedings, for example where the ownership of the underlying rights is contractually complicated or where there are genuinely competing claims to the underlying trade mark. The regulatory bodies will not get involved in a dispute once legal proceedings are under way.

Although the polices of ICANN, EURid and Nominet are not identical, the requirements which must be satisfied are as follows (with those requirements unique to ICANN in **bold**, EURid in *italics* (and common to both in ***bold italics***) and Nominet underlined):

- the respondent's domain name is identical or [***confusingly***] similar to a trade mark or service mark in which the claimant has rights
- [***the respondent has no rights or legitimate interests in respect of the domain name***] and

- the registration [**and use**/*or use*] of the domain
  name is [***in bad faith***/<u>abusive</u>]

Assuming that you can show rights in your trade
mark, you must first show that the domain name
complained of is identical or similar to your mark.
That similarity can be oral, conceptual or pho-
netic, for example kjkrowling.com and eazyjet.
com were found to be confusingly similar to the
more commonly known trade marks JK Rowling
and Easyjet.

Under the ICANN dispute resolution policy you
must then show that the registrant has no legitimate rights in the domain name. This can be a
difficult test to satisfy where, for example, the
website is a complaints site or an enthusiasts' site.
Thus Porsche failed to recover porschebuy.com
where the name was used in good faith for the
online resale of Porsche cars. Although legitimacy
is not a requirement under the Nominet policy, it
is incorporated into the concept of abusive registration such that if the owner did have a legitimate interest in the mark, the registration would
not be abusive.

The crux of any complaint is whether registration
of the domain name is in 'bad faith' (ICANN and
EURid) or 'abusive' (Nominet). Each policy sets
out a non-exhaustive list of circumstances that
will indicate bad faith, including: where the

dominant purpose of the registration is so that the owner can charge an inflated price for the domain name to the trade mark owner; where the owner uses the domain name to obtain commercial gain by misdirecting internet traffic due to confusion with another's mark; or so that the registrant can disrupt the trade mark owner's business.

Although dispute resolution proceedings are less formal than legal proceedings, written complaints should be supported by proof of rights in your trade mark, any evidence of a history of cyber-squatting/disruption of your business, and unfair commercial gain by the registrant.

Chapter

11

....

THE TAKE-HOME MESSAGE

The first thing we do, let's kill all the lawyers.
William Shakespeare, *Henry VI, Part 2*

THE DOS AND DON'TS OF BRAND STRATEGY

To sum up:

	Do	Don't
Trade mark registrations	Consider registering any words, slogans, devices, logos, jingles, shapes, packaging, colouring or labelling that distinguish your goods or services from those of your competitors.	Rely purely upon the law of passing off which requires, in every case, establishing that there is a likelihood of confusion.
	Check the availability of your proposed trade mark by conducting a trade mark search.	Leave your trade mark search until too late: do it at the outset to avoid any wasted marketing costs or subsequent infringement actions against you.

Carefully consider which classes of goods or services need to be covered by your trade mark registration.

Overlook any countries where the brand has a market and which should therefore be covered by trade mark registrations.

Ensure that your applications are consistently made in the name of the same and correct company.

Ever permit distributors or licensees to register your trade mark in their own name.

Ensure that you have a trade mark watching service in place for key trade marks, to ensure that you are notified of competing applications.

Delay once you become aware of a competing application: you only have a short time within which to oppose.

Keep your trade mark certificates in a safe place.

Lose your trade mark certificate!

	Do	Don't
Trade mark portfolios	Maintain and update an accurate record of all of your trade mark registrations and applications. Consider whether any trade mark licences need notifying on the Trade Marks Register. Conduct at the very least annual audits of your trade mark portfolio to determine whether you need to cover any additional classes or territories since first registered, or whether you can let some marks lapse.	Cease using valuable trade marks: non-use for a continuous period of five years will render the trade mark registration liable to revocation.

Monitor renewal dates in your portfolio on a monthly basis.

Overlook any renewal dates: it could cost you your registration.

Only use your trade marks as adjectives, never as nouns or verbs.

Allow your trade marks to develop into generic terms: if they do, they will no longer be registrable as trade marks.

Ensure that you and your licensees/distributors use your trade marks consistently and as registered.

Use variants of your registered trade marks (e.g. plurals, abbreviations, hyphenated, misspelt) unless those variants are also registered as trade marks.

Ensure that any licences or assignments of your trade marks are in writing.

Grant exclusive licences unless you are happy that no other person, including you, can exploit the trade mark in that particular territory.

Do	Don't
Prepare a trade mark usage guide for your commercial people, licensees and distributors, to ensure consistent use of your trade marks in accordance with brand strategy.	Let your licensees or distributors have a free reign on how they use your trade marks.
Regularly educate your board and commercial people, preferably via a written policy, on the importance of and legal issues surrounding your trade marks.	Commission third parties to create trade marks for you without ensuring that the rights are assigned to you.
Have in place an internal chain of command and reporting	

procedure so that everyone knows who is responsible for which trade mark.

Always use the ® symbol with your registered trade marks.

Use the ® symbol if the trade mark is not registered: this is a criminal offence in some jurisdictions. If it is not registered, you can use the ™ symbol.

Protect against parallel imports of grey market goods by:

- including an express term, in your contracts with non-EEA licensees, that they cannot sell your trade marked goods into the EEA

	Do	Don't
	• clearly mark your non-EEA goods as being 'not for resale within the EEA' • applying a unique code to your goods and packaging so that you can identify the licensee and territory to whom you first sold them	
Trade mark infringements	If you are concerned about the importation of infringing goods, notify HM Revenue & Customs who have powers of interception at point of entry.	

Develop good relations with your local Trading Standards Office, who can bring criminal prosecutions against, in particular, counterfeiters.

Consider a criminal complaint to Trading Standards as a possible alternative to civil trade mark infringement proceedings.

Ensure that all of your distributors and licensees are contractually obliged to notify you immediately of any third parties who may be infringing your trade marks.

Forget to notify the relevant person within your organisation with responsibility for that trade mark, as soon as you become aware of a potential infringement.

Do

Seek legal advice as soon as possible.

Ensure that you have an adequate procedure in place to log all examples of consumer/trade confusion between your brand and the potentially infringing mark.

Seek legal advice before making any 'threats' of a trade mark infringement (or patent, UK registered design or UK design right) claim.

Don't

Delay in seeking legal advice: any delay could jeopardise the possibility of stopping the infringer by an injunction.

Design registrations

Check availability of proposed new products by conducting a registered design and patent search.

Consider registering your design (which includes not only products but also device marks, logos, labelling and packaging) as a UK and/or community registered design.

Maintain and update an accurate record of all of your design registrations and applications, noting the renewal dates.

Leave your registered design/patent search until too late: do it at the outset to avoid any wasted development/marketing costs or subsequent infringement actions against you.

Disclose your design to anyone else before applying to have it registered. If you do, it may no longer be novel and may not be registrable.

Do

Ensure that any product incorporating your design is marked clearly with the words 'registered design' and the registration number.

As with trade marks, ensure that in the case of registered design infringements:

- your distributors and licensees are contractually obliged to notify you as soon as they become aware of infringements
- seek legal advice without delay to maximise your chances of obtaining an injunction

Don't

Copyright		
	If you have a good idea, record it in as much detail as possible (e.g. in writing, on a tape), to ensure that you have copyright in it.	Disclose good ideas to third parties without first getting them to sign a confidentiality agreement.
	Ensure that you obtain a written copyright assignment (and possibly a moral rights waiver) from anyone who creates a literary, dramatic, musical or artistic work on your behalf.	Allow your commercial people to commission works from third parties without understanding the potentially adverse copyright ownership implications.
	Conduct regular audits of copyright works essential to your business, e.g. who owns the copyright in your key logos, labels and packaging designs?	Assume that you own copyright works that you have been using for years.

Do	Don't
Be original with creative ideas.	Copy! Using someone else's literary, dramatic, musical or artistic work (e.g. in your advertising or brochures, on your website) without permission will amount to a copyright infringement.
If in doubt, for any new advertising obtain copy clearance from internal or external counsel.	Leave obtaining copy clearance until the day that the campaign goes live.
If you are concerned about the importation of counterfeit goods, notify HM Revenue & Customs who have powers of interception at point of entry.	

Develop good relations with your local Trading Standards Office, who can bring criminal prosecutions in relation to pirated goods.

Consider a criminal complaint to Trading Standards as a possible alternative to civil copyright infringement proceedings.

Always use the © symbol on your copyright works together with the year of first publication and the name of the copyright owner, e.g. 'Copyright 2005 Macfarlanes'.

	Do	Don't
Database right	Maintain separate financial records of the amounts that you have invested in compiling your key databases.	
	Use Trojan horses (i.e. meaningless, bogus data) in your database to assist in establishing whether someone else has had access to or copied it.	
	Consider database right infringement as an alternative to a difficult copyright infringement claim.	

Domain names

Consider how many different variants you wish to register and with which gTLDs or ccTLDs. A WHOIS search will confirm their availability.

Conduct a trade mark search in respect of any new domain name that you intend to apply for.

Consider registering your domain name itself as a trade mark (e.g. www.macfarlanes.com is a registered trade mark).

Maintain and update an accurate record of all of your domain

Let important domain names lapse after their term of two years.

Do

name registrations, noting their renewal dates.

Monitor competing websites: are they using your trade marks as metatags or reproducing your copyright works?

Conduct regular WHOIS searches to see if anyone else has registered a domain name too close to your own.

Don't

Use competitors' trade marks as metatags: to do so may constitute an infringement of their trade marks.

Make blocking registrations to irritate your competitors: that in itself may amount to a trade mark infringement.

INDEX

© symbol 73–4
® symbol 10–11, 85
™ symbol 10–11, 85

absolute grounds, objection
    on 38, 41, 45, 46, 50
abusive domain name
    registration 192
advertising agencies,
    copyright ownership
    17
advertising, copyright 12
Advertising Standards
    Authority 181
Alliance Against
    Counterfeiting &
    Piracy (AACP) 121
alternative dispute
    resolution (ADR)
    159–60
  mediation 159–60
  mini trial 160
  neutral evaluation/
    appraisal 160

annual report, copyright 12
Anti Copying in Design
    (ACID) 122
anti-counterfeiting bodies
    121–2
Anti-Counterfeiting Group
    (ACG) 122
Appellant's Notice 44
Appointed Person, appeal to
    43, 44
artistic works, copyright
    14, 17, 18, 137
assignment 102–4
audit, trade mark 87–9

bad faith
  domain name registration
    192
  trade mark registration
    6
balance of convenience test,
    injunctions 165
Berne Convention 72
Board of Appeal 48

branding consultants,
copyright ownership
17
British Music Rights (BMR)
122
British Phonographic
Industry (BPI) 122
British Video Association
(BVA) 122
broadcasts, copyright 14, 16
brochures/catalogues,
copyright 12
Business Software Alliance
(BSA) 122

cable programme, copyright
16, 18
cease and desist letters
153–4
claim forms 157–8
clearance searches for trade
marks 9
colour marks 4
common law search for
trade marks 9
Community Trade Marks
see trade marks, EC
registrations
Companies House 180
company search 180
Compu-Mark 8
confidentiality agreement,
copyright and 15
confidentiality clauses
95–6
confusion log 151–2, 168
copy clearance 181

copyright 12–20
categories 13–14
international protection
71–3
licences and assignments
16
moral rights 19–20
ownership 15–17
period of protection 18
protecting ideas 15
restrictions on 14
rights of owner 136
in the UK 71
see also copyright
infringement
Copyright Designs &
Patents Act (1988)
118
copyright infringement
civil infringement 136–9
adaptation of work 138
communicating work to
public 138
issuing copies to the
public 137
performing, showing,
playing in public 138
plagiarism 136–7
renting/lending copies
to the public 137–8
criminal offences 140–1
defences to 139–40
cost
appeals, trade mark
registration 44
copyright 12
database right 21

of interim injunctions
167
see also fees
counterfeiting 119
country-code suffixes
(ccTLDs) 185
criminal offences
copyright infringement
140–1
designs 148
trade mark 131–2
cross undertaking in
damages, injunctions
165–6
CTM Bulletin 46
cybersquatters 186, 188,
189
Czech Arbitration Court
190, 191

dance, works of, copyright
14
database right 20–3
definition 20–1
duration 22
infringement 21–2
ownership 22–3
protection 21–2
descriptive marks 5
designs 23–33
benefits of registering
device marks/logos
as 32–3
commissioned 26
criminal offences 148
definition 29
duration of registration 76

employees 26
European Community,
registered 24, 28–31,
147–8
appeal process 78
contesting 78–9
infringement 147–8
registration procedure
77–9
term of protection 30–1
European Community
registration procedure
77–9
European Community,
unregistered 24,
28–31, 147–8
compulsory licensing
148
term of protection 29,
30
individual character 25
infringement 147–8
novelty 25
objections 75–6
overlap between trade
marks and 31–2
product, definition 29
registration procedure
74–6
UK registered 24–6
defences 143–4
infringement 142
registration procedue
74–6
term of protection 26
UK unregistered (design
right) 24, 27–8

compulsory licensing
147
defences 146–7
infringement 144–6
qualification 27–8
term of protection 28
disclosure 158
domain names
alternative dispute
resolution 189–93
Czech Arbitration Court
190–191
disputes 187–8
global suffixes (gTLDs)
184–5, 190
ICANN 190–3
Nominet 190–192
problems with registration
system 185–6
registering 184–5
search 180
trade mark infringement/
passing off claim
188–9
dramatic works, copyright
14, 18, 137
drawings, copyright 14

Easyjet 192
eBay monitoring 124–5
employees
chain of command
99–100
commission work/
contractors 97–8
communicating
importance of 98–9

confidentiality clauses
95–6
copyright ownership and
15
database right and 23
design right and 26, 28, 30
employment contracts
94–5
as IP guardians 125
moral rights 19
moral rights and waiver
96–7
employment contracts 94–5
Entertainment and Leisure
Software Publishers
Association (ELSPA)
122
equitable rights 102
European Court of Justice
(ECJ) 3
Board of Appeal 48
European Economic Area
(EEA) 133–5
goods arriving from
outside 115–16
goods arriving from
within 116–17
European Registry of
Internet Domain
Names (EURid) 190,
191, 192
European Union 29, 49
exhaustion of rights 133

Federation Against
Copyright Theft
(FACT) 122

Federation Against Software
    theft (FAST) 122
fees
    appeal, OHIM,
        Community trade
        mark registrations 48
    CTM applications 44–5
    design
        Community registration
        77
        UK registration 75
    EuRid 191
    HM Revenue and Customs
        116, 117
    ICANN 191
    international trade mark
        49
    Patent Office handling
        fee for OHIM
        application 45
    renewal, trade mark 91
    trade mark registrations
        37
    watching services 121
films, copyright 14, 16, 18
franchising 110–11
freelance writers
    copyright ownership 17
    moral rights 19
freezing injunctions 167

*Gazette of International
    Marks* 50
generic descriptions, trade
    mark restrictions 5
global suffixes (gTLDs
    184–5, 190

goodwill 9, 82, 109, 173
guarantees, order for
    lodging of 168

HM Revenue and Customs
    (R&C) 115–17

ICANN 190–3
illustrations, copyright 14
infringement of intellectual
    property rights
    detecting 114–15
    governmental/public
        agencies for detecting
        115–17
    private service providers
        for monitoring
        119–25
    reason for monitoring 114
    see also infringement of
        intellectual property
        rights, action against
infringement of intellectual
    property rights,
    action against
    alternative dispute
        resolution (ADR)
        159–60
    cease and desist letters
        153–4
    confusion log 151–2, 168
    damages/account of
        profits 171–4
    giving up 161
    interim injunction 151
    litigation 157–9
    mediation 159–60

mini trial 160
neutral evaluation/
    appraisal 160
reporting procedure and
    chain of command
    150
speed of action against
    151
Trading Standards and
    160
unjustified threats
    154–5
website infringements
    and service providers
    155–6
    see also remedies
infringement, inadvertent,
    avoiding 178–81
injunction 114
    breach of 163
    freezing 167
    interim 163–7
    mandatory 162
    permanent 163
    prohibitive 162
    speed of action 165
integrity, right of 19
International Chamber of
    Commerce (ICC)
    Counterfeiting
    Intelligence Bureau
    (CIB) 122
International Federation of
    Phonographc
    Industries (IFPI)
    122

Internet Corporation for
    Assigned Names and
    Numbers (ICANN)
    190, 191, 192
internet searching 179
IP Enforcement Directive
    171
IP Enforcement Regulations
    (April 2006) 171

jingles, copyright 12, 14

labels, copyright 12, 14
licence 102–4
    exclusive/non-exclusive
    16, 104–5
    registration implications
    105–6
    registration by rogue
    licensees 106–7
    standard protective
    licensing provisions
    107–10
    enforcement method
    109
    infringing activities
    108
    rights of approval 108
    scope 107
licence of right 147
literary works, copyright
    12, 13, 18, 137
logos
    benefits of registering as
    designs 32–3
    copyright 12, 13, 14, 17

design right 27
registering as design 24
registering trade marks 3

Madrid Protocol 49, 51
WIPO database 8
'me too' look-alike products 10
mediation 159–60
melodies, copyright 14
metatags 124
mime, copyright 14
mini trial 160
mitigation 173
moral prejudice 172, 173
moral rights
copyright 19
employees 96–7
integrity, right of 19
paternity, right of 19
morality, trade mark restrictions 5
mortgaging IP 112
musical works, copyright 14, 18, 137
must fit exclusion 26, 31
must match exclusion 26, 31

neutral evaluation/appraisal 160
Nice classification of goods and services for trade mark registrations 36–7, 52–71
Nominet 190, 191, 192

Norwich Pharmacal Order 175, 186
Notice of Defence and Counterstatement 41
Notice of Opposition and Statement of Grounds 41, 42

Office for Harmonisation in the Internal Market (OHIM) 44–8, 77, 78, 79
online searches for trade marks 8

paintings, copyright 14
particulars of claim 158
passing off, law of 9–10, 11
Patent Office (UK) 25, 37, 45, 74, 75, 78, 79, 147
Mediation Service Team 160
Patents and Designs Journal 76
paternity, right of 19
photographs, copyright 14, 17
piracy 119
plays, copyright 14
police 119
pre-emptive searches
for registered design/ patent 179–80
for trade marks 6–9, 179
preliminary indication 41–2

private investigators 122–3
public awareness initiatives
        125
published editions,
        copyright 18

registered trade marks
        128–35
    advantages 128
    civil infringement
        128–30
    criminal trade mark
        offences 131–2
    grey market goods
        problem 132–5
    use of 11
registry searches for trade
        marks 8
relative grounds, objection
        on 38, 41, 46, 50
remedies 161–75
    compensation 162–3
    delivery up 161, 169
    destruction 161, 171
    disclosure of identity 162,
        174–5
    injunction 161, 162,
        163–7
    interim order 161
    publication of judicial
        decisions 162, 175
    recall 161, 169–70
    seizure 161, 170
reputation 9, 82, 173
Request to Proceed to the
        Evidential Rounds 42
royal family 6

search orders 167
self-help 123–5
service providers 155–6
shape marks 3, 5
shuttle diplomacy 159–60
slogans, copyright 12
smell marks 3, 4
sound marks 3, 4
sound recordings, copyright
        14, 16, 18
specialist searches, trade
        marks 8
speed
    infringement of
        intellectual property
        rights 151
    injunctions 165
    interim injunctions 168
    trade mark registration 2
    trade mark search 7
syndication 112

test purchases 123–4
theme tunes, copyright 14
third parties
    copyright and 16, 17
    database right and 22–3
    design right and 26, 28,
        30
Trade Descriptions Act
        (1968) 118
trade mark certificate 89
trade mark classes 52–71,
        88
    consistency 89
    territories 89
trade mark notice 10–11, 85

trade mark portfolio, audit
   88
trade mark registration
   certificate 10
Trade Mark Registry (UK)
   49
trade marks 2–11
   accurate and accessible
      records 89–91
   audit 87–9
   avoidance of generic 86–7
   benefits of registering as
      designs 32–3
   categories 3
   consistency in using
      83–6
   duration of protection 32
   EC registrations (CTMs)
      4, 44–8
      appeals 48–9
      application procedure
         44–6
      cooling off period 47
      oppositions 47
      registration 47–8
      term of protection 47
   international registrations
      (Madrid Protocol) 4,
      49–52
   length of registration
      process 41
   Nice classification
      system 36–7, 52–71
   non-traditional 3–4
   opposition 41–2
   overlap between designs
      and 31–2

portfolio 2
pre-emptive searches 6–9,
   37
® and ™ symbols 10–11,
   85
registration 2–4, 42–3
registration in name of
   same proprietor
   82–3
registration period 2
renewal dates 91
restrictions on
   registration 3–5
Registry objections 38–9
UK registrations 4, 37–44
   appeals 43–4
   application procedure
      37–41
   oppositions 40–2
   registration 42–3
   revocation 43
   term of protection 43
Trade Marks Act (1994) 118
Trade Marks Journal 40, 41,
   50
Trade Marks Registry (UK)
   8, 37, 38, 39–44, 91
Trading Standards 118–19,
   123, 140, 160, 181
Trojan horses 23
typographical arrangements
   14, 16
™ symbol, use of 10–11

Union Jack 6
Universal Copyright
   Convention 72, 73

unused IP, mortgaging/
  selling off 111–12

verbal licences 103–4

watching services 119–21
website designers, copyright
  ownership 17

website infringements
  155–6
website monitoring 124
WHOIS search 184, 186
World Intellectual Property
  Organisation (WIPO)
  190
International Bureau 49

Index compiled by Annette Musker